DR. KNOWLEDGE™ PRESENTS

...nge & Fascinating Facts
...bout Famous Brands

DR. KNOWLEDGE™ PRESENTS

Strange & Fascinating Facts About Famous Brands

CHARLES REICHBLUM

Black Dog & Leventhal
Paperbacks

Published by

Black Dog & Leventhal Publishers, Inc.
151 West 19th Street
New York, NY 10011

Distributed by

Workman Publishing Company
708 Broadway
New York, NY 10003

Manufactured in the United States of America

Cover and interior design by Liz Driesbach
Illustrations by George Peters

ISBN: 1-57912-356-2

g f e d c b a

Library of Congress Cataloging-in-Publication Data
is on file at Black Dog & Leventhal Publishers, Inc.

Contents

Dedication

This book is dedicated to the ingenious men and women (and in some cases, young girls and boys) who created the new ideas, conveniences, and products that gave us the famous brands we buy and use today. I'm sure readers like you, along with the listeners of my *Dr. Knowledge*™ radio show, will be just as curious as I was to explore the roots of these beloved products and companies.

How were they conceived? How were they named? What special event may have brought about their births? This book explores the behind-the-scenes, fascinating, and often surprising stories of the brands we know so well.

A lot of people helped "feed" my curiosity. This book is dedicated to them: my wife, Audrey; our children, Bill, Amalie, Bob, and Diane; and our grandchildren, Clarissa, Noah, Justin, and Rachel, who are constantly asking questions (like their grandfather); Black Dog & Leventhal editor Kylie Foxx and literary agent Paula Litzky, who continue to nourish my work; and lastly, to Steve Hansen, Program Director of KDKA radio, who created *The Dr. Knowledge*™ *Show* for listeners whose appetites for answers are as large as my own.

Something to
Snack On

Stroll Down
Chocolate Avenue

There's a town in America named after a popular brand of candy.

Located in the eastern part of the state, Hershey, Pennsylvania, draws thousands of visitors each year and has more than 12,000 permanent residents.

The main street in the town is, naturally, named Chocolate Avenue. It runs perpendicular to Cocoa Avenue. Streetlights are shaped like Hershey's Kisses, and the aroma of chocolate fills the air.

The founder of Hershey, Pennsylvania, and of Hershey candy, was Milton Hershey. Ironically, this man who would eventually become a famous candy maker failed in his first business—running a candy store in Philadelphia. After closing his candy store in 1876, Hershey moved to a dairy farm outside of Harrisburg and began manufacturing milk chocolate bars.

Gradually, Hershey built the largest chocolate factory in the world and became the first to market a candy brand nationally. At the same time, he built a whole town around his factory with homes, schools, and recreational facilities for his employees. (And some very lucky dentists.)

Hershey, Pennsylvania, aptly bills itself as "The Sweetest Place on Earth."

FAST FACT

When Milton Hershey added Hershey's Kisses to his chocolate bar line, there was a debate over what to call the new product. A factory worker looked at the machine making the Kisses and said it looked like the machine was kissing the conveyor belt as it touched the chocolate to give it its distinctive shape. "Hershey's Kisses" they became.

From Field
to Confectionery

Harry Reese and his family lived near Hershey, Pennsylvania, where Hershey chocolates are made. Harry was a farmer who didn't particularly like farming—and he noticed that his neighbor, Milton Hershey, was doing quite well in the candy business.

"If Hershey can make a fortune selling chocolate," Harry reportedly said to his wife one day, "I can at least make a decent living making candy."

Harry had another good reason—actually, sixteen—to try candy. He and his wife had sixteen children, and the idea of manufacturing candy must have been a popular choice in the Reese household.

The Reese Candy Company was born in 1923 in the basement of their home, with Harry and his wife, Blanche, turning out candy in the evenings after farming all day.

Their most popular product grew to be the Reese's Peanut Butter Cup, still a leading seller today. Harry was finally able to retire his hoe entirely.

Harry Reese died in 1956 and the company was sold a few years later to—not surprisingly—the near-by Hershey Chocolate Corporation.

FAST FACT

Tootsie Roll candies were named by their manufacturer, Leo Hirschfield, in 1896, after his six-year-old daughter, Clara, whose nickname was Tootsie.

The Candy with Two Initials for Its Name

The two Ms in M&M candies came from a likely source, the names of the original partners of the manufacturer: Forrest Mars and Bruce Murrie. But the idea for the candies themselves came from a much more unusual place. Would you believe the Spanish Civil War?

Forrest Mars made a trip to Spain during that war in 1937 and saw soldiers eating pellets of chocolate that were encased in a hard sugary coating. The coating prevented the chocolate from melting. Inspired by what he saw, Mars returned to the U.S. and concocted the recipe for M&M's.

First put on the market in 1941, M&M's became a favorite of American GIs in World War II, and by the late 1940s, they were widely available to the public.

The long-lasting M&M's slogan, "The milk chocolate melts in your mouth, not in your hand," debuted on television in 1954, and helped fuel the candy's popularity. Chocolate-covered peanuts were also introduced in the 1950s, along with a myriad of colors added to the original brown.

In 1984 M&M candies rocketed into space—and have been included on shuttle missions ever since.

FAST FACT

The Treat Named After a Day—Almost

In the nineteenth century, some communities set laws against enjoying certain pleasures on Sundays.

Among the things outlawed in Evanston, Illinois, were ice cream sodas. All things with soda were specifically banned on Sundays because they were considered "sinfully good."

But an enterprising storeowner in Evanston got around the law. He came up with a new Sunday treat— ice cream topped by syrup and sauces, but no soda.

The ice cream soda (minus the soda) was originally called an ice cream sunday in honor of the day it was served.

But one more hurdle had to be overcome. Because of the religious disapproval of using the word *Sunday*, the final *y* was changed to *e*, and the ice cream sundae was born. Hooray!

What Country Is Häagen-Dazs Ice Cream From?

It may surprise you to know that Häagen-Dazs ice cream was created, named, and first sold not in any Scandinavian country, as its name might imply, but in the United States.

The story begins in the Bronx area of New York City in the 1920s, when Reuben Mattus worked for his mother and helped to sell her homemade ice cream.

The Mattuses traveled around the Bronx, selling their ice cream from the back of a horse-drawn wagon.

In 1961, Reuben started his own brand of ice cream and wanted a name for it that would convey an aura of old-world tradition. So he made up the name of Häagen-Dazs, which has no particular meaning. It just sounded right.

At first Häagen-Dazs was sold only in gourmet shops around New York City, but sales gradually expanded and it reached national distribution in 1973. The American ice cream with the foreign-sounding name had become a hit.

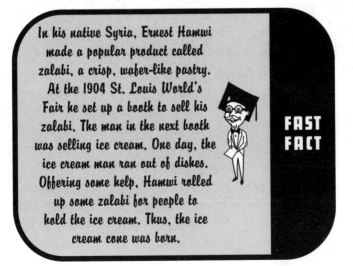

In his native Syria, Ernest Hamwi made a popular product called zalabi, a crisp, wafer-like pastry. At the 1904 St. Louis World's Fair he set up a booth to sell his zalabi. The man in the next booth was selling ice cream. One day, the ice cream man ran out of dishes. Offering some help, Hamwi rolled up some zalabi for people to hold the ice cream. Thus, the ice cream cone was born.

FAST FACT

From Christmas Trees to Song to Movie Title

Borrowing a popular idea from England (where they were called animal cookies), and making a deal with the Barnum circus people, Nabisco introduced Barnum's Animal Crackers to the U.S. in 1902.

To enhance sales, they dressed up the trademark red circus-wagon-shaped box with a string so people could hang them on Christmas trees like ornaments. As clever as that was, kids (and adults) didn't need any inducement to want Animal Crackers. They became a year-round success almost immediately.

Nabisco started with seventeen different animal shapes. More have been added over the years, and for the company's 100th anniversary in 2002, it introduced a fifty-fourth animal (a koala bear).

The influence of Animal Crackers was even reflected in Hollywood. One of the Marx Brothers' hit movies was titled *Animal Crackers*, released in 1930. In the movie, Groucho gave a lecture and delivered the memorable lines, "One morning I shot an elephant in my pajamas. How he got in my pajamas, I'll never know." Animal Crackers also inspired one of Shirley Temple's trademark songs, "Animal Crackers in my Soup" in the 1935 film *Curly Top*.

Caesar Ritz bought a hotel in Paris in the early 1900s, and gave it his name, calling it the Ritz Hotel. It was considered one of the best hotels in the world, and the words "ritz" and "ritzy" entered the language as descriptions of fashionable opulence. The makers of Ritz crackers chose it for their rich, buttery product.

FAST FACT

The World's Best-selling Cookie

After the success of Animal Crackers in the early 1900s, Nabisco tried several other snack products, but none were big hits until, in 1912, they developed a cookie that became the all-time best seller.

It was described by Nabisco as consisting of "two beautifully embossed, chocolate-flavored wafers with a rich cream filling. Twelve flowers are depicted on each side of the cookie." (Still true.)

You've probably guessed its name by now. It was the Oreo, originally called the Oreo Biscuit. Later its name was changed to Oreo Crème Sandwich, and in 1974, Oreo Chocolate Sandwich Cookie.

But why was it called an Oreo?

The name Oreo came from the initial gold-lettered packaging. The French word for gold is *or*—so they became Oreos. They turned out to be good as gold for Nabisco.

The Name Came from a Suburb

It's surprising how many of today's popular snacks date back almost 100 years or more.

Take Fig Newtons, for example. They were invented in 1892 by James Mitchell, who developed a machine that could wrap dough around a filling. He partnered with the Kennedy Biscuit Company in the Boston suburb of Cambridgeport, Massachusetts, and decided to use figs as the filling because he felt they were healthful.

(Yes, a cookie maker concerned for your health.)

But Mitchell and the Kennedy people wondered what they should call the fig cookies.

They decided the name should feature the area where the cookies were made. Fig Cambridgeports

didn't sound too good, and Fig Bostons was rejected. Then, an employee spoke up. He said he lived in
the nearby Boston suburb of Newton, Massachusetts,
and why not pick that name? Fig Newtons they became.

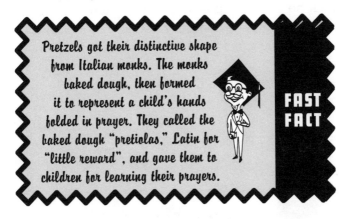

Pretzels got their distinctive shape from Italian monks. The monks baked dough, then formed it to represent a child's hands folded in prayer. They called the baked dough "pretiolas," Latin for "little reward", and gave them to children for learning their prayers.

FAST FACT

Fourteen-year-old's Famous Trademark

Mario Peruzzi and Amedeo Obici, two immigrants
new to America, opened a little fruit and nut stand
in Wilkes-Barre, Pennsylvania, in the early 1900s that
blossomed into a worldwide corporation. Their roast-
ed peanuts were very popular. The men devised a
machine to efficiently make the peanuts in larger
batches, then chose a name for them: Planters Peanuts.

As they began packaging more and more peanuts and enlarging their sales area, Obici and Peruzzi decided in 1916 to sponsor a contest for a good trademark.

The winner was a fourteen-year-old boy, who drew what he called "a peanut person"—a man shaped like a peanut. The company added a monocle, top hat, and cane to the figure, and named him Mr. Peanut. The classy little peanut man has been used ever since, and has become one of the most-recognizable corporate symbols.

What did the fourteen-year-old get for winning the contest? The prize was $5. You might say that was peanuts.

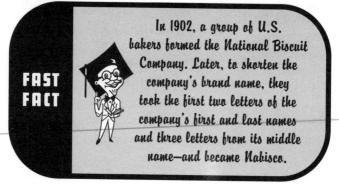

FAST FACT

In 1902, a group of U.S. bakers formed the National Biscuit Company. Later, to shorten the company's brand name, they took the first two letters of the company's first and last names and three letters from its middle name—and became Nabisco.

A Famous Accident

In the early 1900s, kids often made their own soft drinks by mixing flavored soda powder with water.

One evening, eleven-year-old Frank Epperson did just that, but before he could drink it, his mother told him it was time to go to bed. Frank left the drink on his back porch, with a stick he was using to stir it still in the glass.

It turned out to be a very cold night, and when Frank got up the next morning he noticed that his soft drink with a stick in the middle had partially frozen. He pulled the "drink" out of the glass, held it with the stick, and licked it.

Frank never forgot that incident. Eighteen years later, in 1923, he went into business making seven flavors of what he called "Epsicles"—a cross between three letters in his name and "icicle."

But the product never became successful with that name. When Frank's own kids jokingly started referring to the Epsicles as "Pop's icles," Frank decided he preferred that name, and gave the world popsicles.

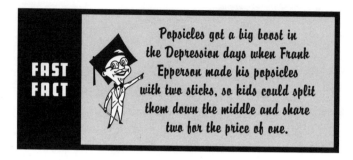

FAST FACT

Popsicles got a big boost in the Depression days when Frank Epperson made his popsicles with two sticks, so kids could split them down the middle and share two for the price of one.

Anger Puts Him Into the Chips

An elegant resort hotel in Saratoga Springs, New York, employed a somewhat temperamental chef named George Crum.

One night in 1853, a dinner guest—the very rich Commodore Cornelius Vanderbilt—complained that Crum's french fried potatoes were too thin and sent them back. Crum apparently didn't like criticism. To spite Vanderbilt, he cut the next order of french fries as thin as possible—so thin and crisp they couldn't be eaten with a fork.

To Crum's surprise, Vanderbilt liked them, and other guests at his table requested more.

Thus, the potato chip was born.

The chips became a specialty of the house—called not potato chips, but Saratoga chips. Later, Crum opened his own restaurant featuring the chips and eventually the chips were packaged and sold, first around upstate New York and then in wider geographic areas.

For many years, even into the 1900s, potato chips were known as Saratoga chips. It took a long time for the potato chip to lose its city of origin.

A New Name Comes Along

A Nashville, Tennessee, food distributor had a small business in 1932. Traveling around the Southeast, he sold items out of the trunk of his car. Among them were potato chips manufactured in Atlanta.

In 1938, he decided to buy out the Atlanta potato chip maker and name their chips after himself. His name was Herman Lay.

Herman expanded the sales of Lay's potato chips and in the 1940s, his company became one of the first to advertise on television. Previously, potato chip brands were sold regionally, but Lay took his brand national. Lay is also credited with the invention of the mechanical potato chip peeler.

Lay's company grew bigger in 1961, when he merged with Texas manufacturer Elmer Doolin, who made Frito corn chips. The new enterprise became today's well-known Frito-Lay company. It joined the Pepsi-Cola company in 1965.

Frito-Lay now also makes popular Doritos, whose name comes from the Spanish phrase for "little bits of gold."

FAST FACT

Nachos were created and named by Ignacio Ahaya. Nacho was Ignacio's nickname.

A New Trend That's Actually Old

Although Krispy Kreme doughnuts didn't arrive on the national scene until the late 1990s and early 2000s, the company was actually founded in 1937.

That year, Vernon Rudolph bought a secret doughnut recipe from a French chef in New Orleans. Rudolph then rented a building in Winston-Salem, North Carolina, and started making Krispy Kremes for local grocery stores.

After a short while, Rudolph opened his own doughnut store and slowly began building a chain in North Carolina and other southern states.

Until Rudolph's death in 1973, Krispy Kremes were sold mainly in the Southeast. The company was sold to Beatrice Foods. A group of investors bought it back from Beatrice in 1976 and began franchising its doughnut stores to a wider region. But it wasn't until the late 1990s that Krispy Kreme entered New York, California, and other states outside the South. The company went public in 2000 and continues to expand nationally and internationally.

WHY TANGERINES?

Tangerines were named after the Moroccan port city of Tangiers. They were first grown in the area around that city in the 1840s.

FAST FACT

Are They Nuts?!

When you stop to think about it, *doughnut* is a funny name for the popular sweet snack. The little round cakes with holes in the center certainly aren't nuts, and they're generally not made with them, so what's with the word *nuts*? (Granted, some people are nutty about doughnuts, but that isn't how they got their name.)

The first American doughnuts were made by the Pilgrims in New England more than 300 years ago. The Pilgrims had learned about the cakes during their stay in Holland. Those original doughnuts were just small pieces of fried dough, without the hole, and were about the size of a walnut.

Since the treats were walnut-sized, and were made of dough, New Englanders started calling them by two words: *dough nuts*.

The name stuck. Over time, people have combined the two words into one, and so today we have doughnuts.

He Was Honored for Inventing Nothing

Hanson Gregory is honored as the inventor of nothing. The "nothing" refers to the hole in doughnuts.

As mentioned, doughnuts originally had no hole in the center. But Gregory, a sea captain from Rockport, Maine, is credited as the first to create doughnuts with that distinctive hole—and he did it for a very practical reason.

Gregory loved to eat doughnuts while piloting his ship. Instead of having the cakes slide all around while the ship was going through rough waters, he put a hole in his doughnuts so he could place them on a spike near his steering wheel.

Gregory's 1847 culinary contribution is commemorated in his hometown with a bronze plaque.

"Cool" by Any Other Name

The Cracker Jack brand was debuted at the Chicago World's Fair in 1893 by German immigrant F. W. Rueckheim.

Rueckheim had a little shop in downtown Chicago where he sold popcorn, candy, and peanuts. With the fair coming to Chicago, he decided to rent a booth and introduce a new product there. Rueckheim took his popcorn and peanuts, added a caramel coating, and created Cracker Jack.

But why that name?

A popular expression in those days for anything good was "crackerjack." People would say, "That's cracker-jack," much like people today say, "That's awesome."

When a salesman sampled Rueckheim's creation and said, "That's crackerjack," Rueckheim had the name he was looking for. He trademarked it, changing the expression into two words.

For the now-famous design on the package, he portrayed his eight-year-old grandson and the boy's dog.

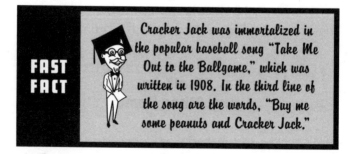

FAST FACT

Cracker Jack was immortalized in the popular baseball song "Take Me Out to the Ballgame," which was written in 1908. In the third line of the song are the words, "Buy me some peanuts and Cracker Jack."

The Sales Idea That Made Millions

Edward Noble made one sales call that would revolutionize marketing.

In 1913, Noble was a struggling salesman who scraped together $2,900 to buy an equally struggling product called Life Savers from Clarence Crane of Cleveland. Crane hadn't done much with his Life Savers because his main business was making chocolate candies.

Noble believed his new acquisition just needed some smart promotion. He made a fateful sales call to the head of United Cigar Stores and convinced him to put a five-cent price card on the Life Savers and to place them near the cash register in the company's 1,200 stores. He also urged all cashiers to give every customer a nickel in change.

The results were spectacular, and began the now-common marketing practice of manufacturers vying for space near the checkout point.

And how did the candies get their unusual name? Well, the original product consisted exclusively of white mints with a hole in the middle; they resembled the lifesavers that are tossed off boats to rescue people overboard.

Noble later added colors—and the company was a lifesaver for him.

FAST FACT

In 1943, the National Broadcasting Company owned two networks, NBC Red and NBC Blue. The federal government stepped in and told NBC to sell one of their networks. Enter Edward Noble. With his Life Saver millions, he bought NBC Blue, and changed its name to the American Broadcasting Company, now known as ABC.

One Smart Cookie

A toll road was built between Boston and New Bedford, Massachusetts, in the early 1700s. Along the road, near the town of Whitman, were a tollgate and house where travelers could stay overnight.

The old house by the toll road was purchased in the late 1920s by Ruth Wakefield, who renovated it into a more modern inn. Ms. Wakefield not only ran the inn, but she did all the cooking for her guests, too. And she loved to make cookies. One day in the

1930s she got the idea of chopping up some chocolate bars into little pieces and putting the pieces into her cookies. Legend has it that Ruth created the first chocolate chip cookies.

Visitors at the inn liked those cookies, and their popularity spread. By the end of the 1930s they became a national hit.

What did Mrs. Wakefield call her chocolate chip cookies?

She had named her inn by the old toll road the Toll House Inn, so her cookies naturally became Toll House cookies.

Holy Health Food

A Presbyterian clergyman from West Suffield, Connecticut, took to his pulpit in the early 1800s and began preaching about what he called the glory of healthful eating.

He told his parishioners they should eat no meat or fish or poultry, and he particularly railed against refined flour in commercial breads and pastries. He said it was a sin to alter the natural foods that God gave us.

As the minister's fiery sermons began to attract a following, he became a controversial figure, and the controversy even led to violence. One night the preacher was attacked by a mob of Boston bakers who didn't like his stand against their breads and pastries.

But one nearby baker joined the clergyman's cause instead of fighting it. In 1829, this baker developed a cracker made with unaltered wheat flour, much to the clergyman's delight.

The baker named his cracker after the minister.

The minister was the Reverend Sylvester Graham, who became the inspiration for graham flour—and the graham cracker.

Baby Gift Grows Up

More than 200 years ago, Jewish people in Poland had a tradition.

After a woman gave birth to a child, she was given gifts of doughnut-shaped rolls for her baby to use as teething rings. They were named after the Yiddish word *beygel*, derived from the Old German *bougel*, which meant bracelet, or ring.

In addition to the beygels for babies, Jewish bakers in Eastern Europe made beygels for the general population to enjoy, too.

When many Polish Jews emigrated to the United States in the late 1800s, they brought their love of beygels with them.

Soon, the name beygels was anglicized to bagels, but their popularity was largely confined to the New York City area. As late as the mid-1900s, most of the U.S. hadn't yet discovered these satisfying, doughy treats.

It wasn't until the 1980s that a large number of bakeries and retail stores brought bagels to mainstream America, and the old baby gift grew up.

The word "pizza" in Italian means pie.

FAST FACT

It's Not Over 'til the Fat Lady Eats?

Melba toast got its name from Australian opera singer Nellie Melba.

Nellie was forever watching her weight. While on tour in England in the late 1800s, she asked the chef at her hotel to serve her toast at breakfast every morning and to make it as thin as possible.

The chef happened to be the famous Escoffier, and he went out of his way to personally see that Nellie's toast was as thin as it could be.

Other guests seemed to like the thin toast and Escoffier named it after Ms. Melba.

But Melba wasn't Nellie's real last name. She was actually born with Mitchell, but she adopted Melba as her stage name to honor her hometown of Melbourne, Australia.

One other dish was named for Nellie. Escoffier created a special dessert for a party to celebrate her opening night. The ice-cream-and-peaches concoction was named Peach Melba, and was at the other end of the scale for the weight-conscious Nellie.

Accidental Fortune

William Wrigley Jr.'s first job was selling soap manufactured by his father's company. A hot-shot salesman, William (known as Junior) got the idea of offering free gifts to merchants as an extra incentive to stock Wrigley Soap on their shelves. The free gifts were cans of baking powder, and he found they were more popular than his dad's soap.

Wanting to go out on his own, Junior, at age 30, decided to leave his father and start a baking powder business in Chicago. Once more, he gave away gifts—this time to stores that bought his baking powder. The gifts were packages of chewing gum. Again, the gifts were more popular than the product they were supposed to promote.

So, a year later, in 1893, young Wrigley switched gears once again, forming a chewing gum company. He called his first gum Wrigley's Juicy Fruit—and that was the beginning of the world's most successful chewing gum enterprise.

With Two Structures, He Brands More Than a Product

In 1920, with Wrigley's chewing gum now a leading brand, founder William Wrigley Jr. decided to build a spectacular building for his company's headquarters. He built a Chicago landmark, and his building began the development of the North Michigan Avenue district, now known as the "Magnificent Mile."

Naturally, he called his contribution the Wrigley Building—but that's not the only structure that carries his name. After buying the Chicago Cubs baseball team, he changed the name of their ballpark in 1916 from its original Weeghman Park to Wrigley Field.

As Wrigley Field, the ballpark has become one of the most famous and beloved baseball venues in the country. The only thing is, the Wrigleys don't own Wrigley Field anymore.

They sold the team—and the ballpark—to the Chicago Tribune Company in 1981. The Tribune didn't want to tinker with tradition, so they kept the Wrigley moniker. Think of all the free publicity the chewing gum still gets.

FAST FACT

Elizabeth Wrigley-Field was born in Los Angeles, grew up in New York, and is not a baseball fan, but her mother's maiden name is Wrigley (no relation to the chewing-gum Wrigleys), and her father's last name is Field. Her parents called her, simply, Elizabeth Field, but Elizabeth thought it'd be cool to take her mother's name, too, so she legally changed her name to Elizabeth Wrigley-Field. Oddly, when she started using her new name, she had never been inside baseball's Wrigley Field.

Checkout Changer

Shopping history was made on June 26, 1974, at Marsh Supermarket in Troy, Ohio.

A ten-pack of Wrigley's Juicy Fruit was run through a laser scanner. The scanner read a newly-created code, called the UPC, or Universal Product Code, on the back of the gum's package, and the register showed a sale of 67¢.

With that, the computerized shopping era began.

Since that first pack of gum, the ubiquitous bar codes have helped sell billions of items and speed millions of shoppers through checkout lines.

Those UPC bar codes, which are a series of lines, identify the manufacturer, product category, the product itself, and the price. They not only quicken the checkout process but also help stores keep track of inventory. The bar code system is also designed to prevent clerks from making mistakes on prices.

After that first pack of chewing gum went through the process in 1974, computerization in stores spread rapidly. Many stores today won't stock items that don't have a bar code.

2

Let's Get Personal
HYGIENE AND HEALTH

Something to Ease the Pain

It wasn't any marketing or focus group that came up with one of the best-known brand names in the world. Chemists at the Bayer company in Germany coined the name aspirin all by themselves in 1899.

To achieve the name, they took the *a* from the first letter of *acetylsalicylic acid*, the product's scientific name. *Spir* came from the first four letters of the Latin word *spiraea*, which describes the plant in the rose family that was the original source of the compound's pain-relieving, fever-lowering, anti-inflammatory qualities. The *in* was added because it was a common suffix at that time for medications.

Alas, after creating aspirin, Bayer lost the exclusive rights to the name (with a capital *A*) after Germany's defeat in World War I. Germany surrendered the brand name to the United States, England, France, and Russia as part of its reparations. Then in a court decision in 1921, Judge Learned Hand ruled that since the drug was so well known, no manufacturer could own its name, and anyone could make it and call it *aspirin*.

He Was Just Trying to Help His Dad— and He Created a Famous Medicine

In the 1890s, twenty-five-year-old Felix Hoffmann had just graduated magna cum laude from the University of Munich with a doctorate degree in chemistry when he began his search for a drug to alleviate his father's arthritis.

Hoffmann investigated some previous work on acetylsalicylic acid that had been done in France forty years before but largely forgotten since. The acid was known to relieve pain, but nobody did anything with it commercially.

In 1897, after joining the Bayer company upon a recommendation from his university professor,

Hoffmann created a chemically pure and stable form of acetylsalicylic acid and tried it on his dad.

It worked.

Bayer then conducted tests on the drug that proved its worth. Two years later, it was put on the market. Bayer—and Hoffmann—had given the world aspirin.

Hoffmann continued to work for Bayer until retiring in 1928. He lived until 1946, out of the public eye and largely unknown by the millions of thankful aspirin users everywhere.

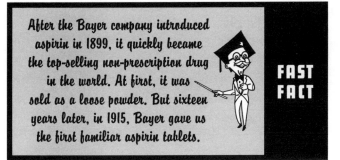

After the Bayer company introduced aspirin in 1899, it quickly became the top-selling non-prescription drug in the world. At first, it was sold as a loose powder. But sixteen years later, in 1915, Bayer gave us the first familiar aspirin tablets.

FAST FACT

Johnson & Johnson & . . . Johnson?

Robert, James, and Edward Johnson formed a company in 1885 under the name of Johnson & Johnson.

Which of the three brothers' last name was left out of the corporate title has never been disclosed, but apparently they felt that three Johnsons in their name would be too long.

The company prospered and today owns many well-known products, including aspirin's leading competitor, Tylenol.

Tylenol has been around since 1965. It works like aspirin but was developed for those whose stomachs are irritated by aspirin. Its active ingredient is acetaminophen, as opposed to aspirin's acetylsalicylic acid.

The makers of Tylenol say it is effective because it elevates the body's pain threshold in order to relieve pain, and helps the body eliminate excess heat in order to lower fever.

Since Tylenol's introduction, Johnson & Johnson figures that more than 240 billion tablets have been taken around the world.

A Little Bit Accident Prone

Earle Dickson, a cotton buyer at Johnson & Johnson

pharmaceuticals, married Josephine Knight in 1920.

Life was good, but there was one problem.

Though married life agreed with Josephine, house-keeping did not. The newlywed kept having minor accidents in the kitchen, frequently getting cuts and burns on her fingers. With no ready-made bandages available then, Josephine had no easy way of tending to her own wounds. Many evenings Earle would come home and prepare bandages for Josephine.

At last, he decided to make some do-it-yourself bandages for his young wife. Earle cut pieces of adhesive tape and placed small squares of cotton and gauze on them, then covered the sticky portions with crinoline. Now all Josephine had to do was strip off the crinoline and wrap the little bandages over her cuts.

Earle told his bosses about his invention and they were intrigued. They set about designing and manufacturing Earle's idea. Just one year later, the self-help bandages were ready for the market. Johnson & Johnson called them Band-Aids. Since then, the company says it has made more than 100 billion of the handy little strips.

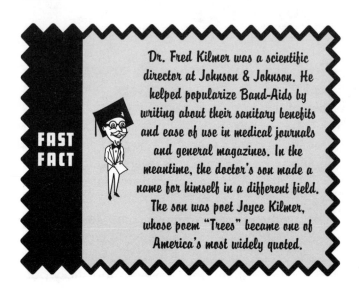

FAST FACT

Dr. Fred Kilmer was a scientific director at Johnson & Johnson. He helped popularize Band-Aids by writing about their sanitary benefits and ease of use in medical journals and general magazines. In the meantime, the doctor's son made a name for himself in a different field. The son was poet Joyce Kilmer, whose poem "Trees" became one of America's most widely quoted.

Plop, Plop, Fizz, Fizz

An old home remedy was the inspiration for the successful launch of a new product.

Hub Beardsley, head of Miles Laboratories, heard about a newspaper editor who advocated taking a combination of aspirin and baking soda at the first sign of a cold. The editor reported that none of his employees missed a day's work during cold and flu epidemics because they practiced his aspirin-and-baking-soda regimen.

Beardsley asked his chief chemist, Maurice Treneer,

to experiment with a tablet that would incorporate the so-called magic combination. Testing of Treneer's tablet showed that it not only helped colds but was also good for headaches, seasickness, and hangovers.

Miles launched the tablets in 1931 under the name Alka-Seltzer, and with heavy advertising it became a popular product. Part of its success was credited to its famous "Plop, Plop, Fizz, Fizz" campaign.

That fizzing also prompted a national joke by movie star and radio personality W. C. Fields. Many heavy drinkers had begun taking Alka-Seltzer for hangovers, and Fields, who was known for his own tippling habit, reportedly plopped two tablets in a glass of water, heard the fizz, and was quoted as saying, "Can't anybody do something about that racket?!"

Although the original success of Alka-Seltzer was based on its one-two combination of aspirin and baking soda, the company later realized that aspirin causes stomach sensitivity in some people. Forty years after its introduction, some Alka-Seltzer products are now available aspirin free.

FAST FACT

Wife's Flower Vases Become Basis for Brand Name

In 1859, a struggling Brooklyn, New York, chemist, Robert Chesebrough, read about the first U.S. commercial oil well—located in Titusville, Pennsylvania—and all the trouble an oil residue was causing workers there.

The residue was sticking to the oil drills, gumming up the pumping. Workers had to remove it by hand. But while doing that, they noticed it soothed the many cuts and burns they had.

Chesebrough decided to visit Titusville and bring home some samples.

He experimented with the residue, intentionally cutting and burning himself, then applying the oily substance to his wounds. He confirmed it had healing powers and thus began making what he called "petroleum jelly."

But he wanted a better name.

Inspiration was in his kitchen. While extracting and purifying the residue's ingredients, he used his wife's flower vases as beakers. Chesebrough looked at the vases, and came up with "Vase" for the first part of the name, then added "line," which was a popular ending for medicines at the time. Thus, Chesebrough gave the world Vaseline petroleum jelly.

One Product, Many Uses

Vaseline came out in 1870. Its inventor, Robert Chesebrough, was ninety-six when he passed away in 1933, so he had many years to enjoy his success.

Although Chesebrough invented Vaseline as a healing product, he was surprised and happy to learn of all the other uses people found for it. It can help prevent rusting in machinery, polish and protect wood surfaces, revive dried leather, inhibit corrosion, remove stains from wood furniture, and protect skin from chapping.

Chesebrough also heard that long-distance swimmers smeared it on their bodies, baseball players used it to break in their gloves, and skiers used it to protect their faces from the cold.

But perhaps Chesebrough was the most devoted to Vaseline. He ate a spoonful of his invention every day and claimed it was the secret for his longevity.

Tummy Trouble

In the basement of his St. Louis drugstore in 1928, Jim Howe concocted a mint-flavored antacid tablet from calcium carbonate for his wife, who often suffered from indigestion.

Howe kept the tablets in an old mason jar and gave them to his wife as needed. She liked them, and they seemed to work.

Eventually, Howe teamed up with his uncle, A. H. Lewis, who was a pharmacist in Bolivar, Missouri. In 1930, they formed the Lewis Howe company to make and sell Jim's antacid tablets.

Lewis and Howe ran a radio contest to come up with a name for their product. A nurse in St. Louis County, thinking of tummy relief, suggested TUMS.

The slogan and advertising campaign that logically followed was, "TUMS for the tummy." It became one of the best-known brand slogans and helped popularize the product.

Although Howe and Lewis eventually sold their company (as of 2004, the product is made by GlaxoSmithKline), TUMS are still manufactured in the same red brick building in downtown St. Louis that was used in 1930.

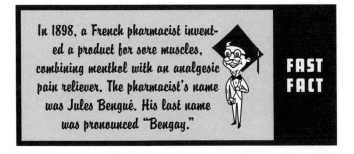

In 1898, a French pharmacist invented a product for sore muscles, combining menthol with an analgesic pain reliever. The pharmacist's name was Jules Bengué. His last name was pronounced "Bengay."

FAST FACT

The King Who Changed Shaving

The man who changed the world's shaving habits was a King—but he wasn't a member of royalty.

He was named King Camp Gillette, born in Fond du Lac, Wisconsin, in 1855. King Gillette became a traveling salesman, and settled in Brookline, Massachusetts. While on the road selling bottle cap stoppers for carbonated beverages, Gillette dreamed of creating his own product—one that people would use, throw away, and replace often (which, of course, would drive sales).

For years he carried that dream, but couldn't come up with the right idea. Finally in 1895, the inspiration hit Gillette while he was shaving with the straight-edge razor then in vogue.

It took Gillette eight years to raise money to develop his idea of a safety razor with thin, disposable blades. His product went on the market in 1903. He only sold fifty-one razors and 168 blades that first year, but as word spread, sales quickly picked up and a shaving revolution had begun.

By 1906, Gillette sold 300,000 razors and 12 million blades. Eventually, more than 1 billion people around the world would use Gillette's products every day.

This King ruled the shaving world.

A Cold Snap

During World War I, Jacob Schick was a U.S. soldier stationed in Alaska. When he went to shave one morning, he found no hot water. Schick began to think about creating a way a person could shave without using water.

He came up with the idea of an electric razor, but it took years for him to develop what he called a "dry shaver."

Schick worked day after day to perfect a small

electric motor that would be practical. Meanwhile, he mortgaged his home and sank into debt.

Finally, thirteen years after World War I, in 1931, Schick had raised enough money to bring the world's first electric razor to market.

It was a tough sell during the Great Depression, but Schick prevailed and gave people a new way to shave.

Why They're Called Soap Operas

Oxydol laundry soap started something new in 1933. They began sponsoring a daily fifteen-minute afternoon drama on network radio. Their program was called *Ma Perkins.*

It was popular, and soon other soap brands decided to sponsor the same kind of show. The airwaves became full of afternoon dramas aimed at a predominately female audience. The phrase "soap operas" entered the language to describe these soap-sponsored programs.

Some long-running soap operas of that era included *Stella Dallas, Portia Faces Life, Just Plain Bill, Life Can Be Beautiful, The Guiding Light, Our Gal Sunday,* and *Backstage Wife.*

(Incredibly, Virginia Payne, who played Ma on *Ma Perkins,* held that role for the entire twenty-seven-year run of the program—never missing any of its 7,065 broadcasts.)

It Floats–
by Accident

Two history-making foreigners emigrated to the U.S. in the early 1800s: William Procter from England, and James Gamble from Ireland. Both settled in Cincinnati, Ohio, where Procter got a job as a candlemaker and Gamble worked for a soap manufacturer.

They didn't know each other and might never have met had they not married sisters, Olivia and Elizabeth Norris. Their mutual father-in-law, Alexander Norris, suggested that his new sons-in-law go into business together—making candles and soap.

They each put in $3,500 in 1837 and formed a partnership called Procter & Gamble. The two brothers-in-law prospered making their candles and soap, but the company's big breakthrough came forty-one years later, in 1878, when one of their workers forgot to turn off the soap-making machine when he left for lunch.

When the worker returned, he found there was too much air in the soap. But it seemed to be a good thing! All the excess air made the soap float. History's first floating soap bars had been created—by mistake—and became an instant hit. Procter & Gamble was swamped with orders by people seeking soap that would stay atop the water in the tub instead of sinking to the bottom.

Divine Inspiration

Harley Procter, son of Procter & Gamble's co-founder, William Procter, wanted a distinctive name for the company's new floating soap.

In church one Sunday morning, Harley was thinking more about his soap than the minister's sermon. But as the clergyman read the Forty-fifth Psalm, one word jumped out to Harley. The minister intoned, "All thy garments smell of myrrh, and aloes, and casina, out of the ivory palaces, whereby they have made thee glad."

"That's it," Harley said to himself. "Ivory." Procter & Gamble had always advertised their soap as pure and white, so it was the perfect tie-in.

The first bars of the newly named soap went on sale in 1879, but Harley's brainstorming wasn't done.

Hoping to take advantage of the soap's supposed purity, he sent some bars to an independent laboratory for testing. The lab reported the soap had 56/100 of 1 percent impurities. Harley flipped that around and advertised that Ivory Soap was 99.44 percent pure.

That slogan—along with "It Floats"—became among the most successful ad campaigns of all time.

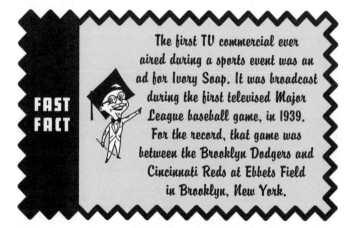

FAST FACT

The first TV commercial ever aired during a sports event was an ad for Ivory Soap. It was broadcast during the first televised Major League baseball game, in 1939. For the record, that game was between the Brooklyn Dodgers and Cincinnati Reds at Ebbets Field in Brooklyn, New York.

Make Your Own Soap

Of all the major brands of consumer products today, which one is the oldest?

The one that's been available for the longest continuous time is Colgate.

That company, today called Colgate-Palmolive after a merger with Palmolive, was founded in 1806 by William Colgate, who emigrated to America from England and set up a soap and candle business in New York City.

Colgate was one of the first soap makers in the United States. It may seem hard to believe, but until the 1800s many people made their own soap. And it was not a simple process. They had to pour hot water over wood ashes to make potash, then boil that with animal fats or vegetable oils, and let the mixture harden.

Colgate and other soap makers who began springing up in the 1800s gradually diminished the custom of soap making at home, and customers welcomed the change. To separate itself from the competition, Colgate was the first to add perfume to its soap. It proved to be a big hit. They called their perfumed soap Cashmere Bouquet.

Soaps are made up of molecules that attach themselves to dirt and germ particles, and hold onto them until water rinses them away.

FAST FACT

To Bathe
or Not to Bathe

Just as it's hard to imagine most people making their own soap, it's surprising to learn that there were times in human history when it was felt—or decreed—that people should not wash their bodies.

Some early religions said that exposing one's skin to washing was a sin. They strictly forbade their followers from taking baths.

Even doctors at times advised against bathing. During the Middle Ages there were medical theories that water and soap opened one's pores and let diseases in.

To combat body odor, fashionable people doused themselves with perfume instead of washing.

On top of all that, indoor plumbing was not common until the nineteenth century, so you had to either bathe outside or bring a tub inside and fill it with water. Since modern bathrooms didn't exist in many homes until the late 1800s, it was not unusual to take a bath in the kitchen.

As late as the twentieth century, a once-a-week Saturday night bath was the norm for many.

(Luckily history books aren't scratch 'n' sniff.)

You Might Have Preferred "Morning Mouth"

Two thousand years ago, people brushed their teeth with all sorts of things, including human urine.

Early Roman physicians felt that urine had special qualities for whitening teeth and preventing decay. Other civilizations used a combination of strong vinegar and powdered pumice stone. There were many kinds of homemade "toothpastes"—few of which tasted very good or were very good for teeth or gums.

It wasn't till the twentieth century that manufacturers began making pleasant-tasting toothpastes. Early brands included Colgate, Pepsodent, and Ipana.

A major breakthrough occurred when scientists discovered that many people living in the vicinity of Naples, Italy, had no cavities. It was determined that water in that area was extremely high in fluoride. Cities in the United States began treating their water with fluoride, and a toothpaste maker took notice.

In 1955, Procter & Gamble introduced the first toothpaste with fluoride, Crest. It rose to No. 1 in popularity on the strength of an endorsement by the American Dental Association.

We've come a long way from the early toothpastes.

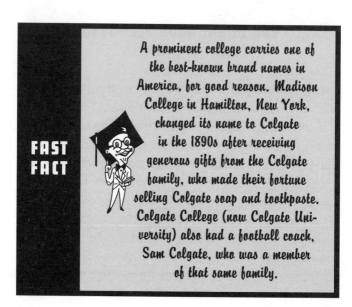

FAST FACT

A prominent college carries one of the best-known brand names in America, for good reason. Madison College in Hamilton, New York, changed its name to Colgate in the 1890s after receiving generous gifts from the Colgate family, who made their fortune selling Colgate soap and toothpaste. Colgate College (now Colgate University) also had a football coach, Sam Colgate, who was a member of that same family.

The Surprise About Toilet Paper

Would you believe there was no commercially made toilet paper in the civilized world until the late 1800s?!
The history of bathrooms in general has not gotten much coverage over the years (maybe that's a

good thing?), and many people are surprised to learn that even the wealthy did not have such luxuries as toilet tissue and indoor plumbing.

Just about everybody then used outhouses, which were stocked with plenty of reading materials like old newspapers, mail-order catalogs, and assorted advertising fliers. The reading materials were used as toilet paper.

Many outhouses were nothing more than primitive little shacks. Sanitation, comfort, heat, and other modern niceties were absent.

About the same time that indoor plumbing was becoming an option in the 1800s, two brothers, Edward and Clarence Scott of Philadelphia, manufactured the first rolls of paper specifically for bathroom use. They called their wonder-paper Scott's Tissue, a euphemistic name still used on packages today.

Although the 1800s saw the creation of indoor plumbing, it took almost a century for it to become prevalent.

FAST FACT

FAST FACT

SHARE AND SHARE ALIKE
As indoor bathrooms became possible, big-city hotels were among the first to have them, but they weren't quite the same as today. At first, hotels did not have private bathrooms in each room. The few bathrooms available, often one to a floor or located in the basement, were meant to be shared. Hotel guests had to line up and wait their turn.

Why the "Q" in Q-tips?

One day in 1923, Leo Gerstenzang observed his wife attaching cotton to a toothpick, and a new product was born.

Gerstenzang owned a company that made baby-care accessories, and he realized a small stick with cotton on it would be perfect for mothers to use on their babies.

The product went through several name changes. It was originally called Baby Gays. Then Gerstenzang made it Q-tips Baby Gays. Finally, in 1926, he dropped "Baby Gay" altogether.

By that time it was obvious that Q-tips had more uses than just for babies. Adults began using the cotton swabs to clean their own ears, and to clean small spaces and equipment around the house.

But why the Q in Q-tips?

Gerstenzang explained that he used only 100 percent pure cotton and the Q stood for quality. He trademarked it and a new word entered the language.

A New Way to Honk Your Horn

Kleenex tissues originally had nothing to do with nose blowing.

Kimberly-Clark manufactured the tissues as filters for gas masks during World War I. After the war, they still had a supply of the tissues with no way to sell them in any great quantity.

They began to advertise what they called Kleenex Kerchiefs as cold cream removers for women. But a funny thing happened.

Kimberly-Clark heard that people were using the cold cream removers as disposable handkerchiefs. Some women wrote the company to complain that their husbands were using their Kleenex Kerchief tissues to blow their noses.

So Kimberly-Clark ingeniously started an ad campaign in the early 1930s, promoting Kleenex as disposable handkerchiefs. It became so popular as a brand name that Kleenex emerged as a virtual generic word for all facial tissues, even those made by other manufacturers. However, Kimberly-Clark still owns the trademark for Kleenex—whose main use was discovered by chance.

Does She or Doesn't She?

Until the 1950s, the vast majority of women did not change the color of their hair, and many thought it was improper to do so. People often looked down upon those who did.

The hair-color revolution was sparked by a Clairol advertising campaign that asked, "Does she or doesn't she?" The ads portrayed so-called respectable women who had supposedly changed the color of their hair. But *Life* magazine, then a major advertising medium, as well as some TV stations, refused to run the ads because they thought the question was too suggestive.

To get the ads running, Clairol asked *Life* to survey their female employees about whether they were offended by the ad. None said they were, so *Life* accepted the ads and the campaign took off. Clairol began racking up record sales.

That 1950s campaign plus the burgeoning women's movement and youth rebellion of the 1960s gave women (and men) of all ages the freedom to change their hair color without stigmatization.

Beauty and the Bard

There *is* a connection between William Shakespeare and the well-known Avon ladies who sell Avon products.

Twenty-eight-year-old David McConnell started a business of selling books door to door in 1886. As an inducement for women to buy his books, McConnell gave away free bottles of perfume that he and a druggist friend made on the side. McConnell soon found his customers wanted the perfume more than the books. He switched to selling the perfume and founded the California Perfume Company.

It took him fifty years, but in 1936, McConnell decided to change the company's name. The name he chose was a tribute to his favorite playwright; you know, that famous guy from Stratford-on-Avon. California Perfume became Avon Products.

By that time, the company had expanded to include various cosmetics lines, and employed what became known as Avon ladies to call on homes around the world.

There Was No Chanel No. 1, 2, 3, or 4

When French fashion designer Gabrielle "Coco" Chanel brought out her line of perfume in 1921, she purposely staged the introduction on the fifth day of the fifth month (May 5) because she was superstitious and considered five to be her lucky number.

And, even though there weren't four versions that preceded it, her perfume was named Chanel No. 5, to commemorate its introduction day and satisfy her belief in a lucky number.

As it turned out, it *was* lucky for Coco Chanel. Her perfume became one of the best-known brands in the world, and she made millions from it.

The story of Chanel—the woman, not the perfume—became a hit Broadway musical in 1970. The show, called "Coco," starred Katharine Hepburn as Chanel.

Another Hollywood actress, Marilyn Monroe, helped publicize Chanel in a different way. A reporter asked Monroe a question, and her answer appeared in newspapers everywhere. The reporter inquired of Monroe what she wore to bed every night. Monroe replied, coyly, "Chanel No. 5."

A City or a Saint?

The company that now makes St. Joseph's aspirin, McNeil, offers two explanations for the brand's name.

They surmise it came either from the patron saint of families, children, and the sick, St. Joseph, or from the city of St. Joseph, Missouri, where the founder had been successful in an early business deal.

The problem with finding the brand's origin is that it was created long ago, in the 1800s, by Leo Gerstile of the Gerstile Medicine company. Gerstile wasn't from St. Joseph—he lived in Chattanooga, Tennessee—but apparently made a big sale in the Missouri city, creating the legend for the product's name. On the other hand, Gerstile was thought to be a religious man, so naming it after a saint would have been logical.

The aspirin was unique in that it was specially designed for youngsters. It contained only 81 milligrams of acetylsalic acid, as opposed to the 325 milligrams in regular adult aspirin.

In an interesting development, many adults now take baby aspirin for their heart conditions. In fact, St. Joseph's is now advertised for grownups as well.

3

Fun for the Whole Family

Flying Disks

Were Frisbees Named After a Mr. Frisbee?
Yes and no.

There was a William Frisbie who founded a bakery in southern Connecticut and sold pies in round tin pans embossed with his name.

In the1940s, some students at nearby Yale University were looking for a new kind of recreation, and got the idea of tossing the pie pans around campus just for fun.

That might have been the end of the story, except for a toy manufacturer's visit to Yale.

The manufacturer was Richard Knerr, the head of a California company named Wham-O.

When Knerr visited New Haven, Connecticut, on a business trip, he saw the Yalies throwing the pie pans and realized he had an idea for a new toy. The students called the pie pans Frisbies after Mr. Frisbie's pie company; Knerr adopted the name but changed it slightly. He spelled it *Frisbee*, and trademarked it. Knerr then took his Frisbees, mass-produced and promoted them, and made Frisbees a national craze.

He Lost His Job—
But Made a Fortune

Charles Darrow of Philadelphia lost his job as an engineer during the Depression in the early 1930s. But that brush with misfortune turned out to be a very lucky break.

When Darrow couldn't find another job, he began passing his idle hours devising board games at his kitchen table. His family and neighbors especially seemed to enjoy one game in particular; Darrow decided to focus on it and and refine it.

Darrow was running out of money, so he got a vicarious thrill out of creating play-money for his game, and buying high-priced real estate. His game, as you may have guessed, was Monopoly. For the game board's street locations, he used the street names in Atlantic City, New Jersey, a town he used to visit during more affluent times.

In 1934, Darrow took his game to a leading game manufacturer, Parker Brothers. Monopoly went on to become one of the best-selling, most continuously popular board games of all time.

The formerly unemployed Charles Darrow became a wealthy man. Had he not been unemployed, he might never have made it.

A man with four names—George Washington Gale Ferris—gave his last name to Ferris wheels. Ferris was an American engineer who specialized in bridge construction. He built the first Ferris wheel for use at the Chicago World's Fair in 1893. The wheel was 250 feet high and could carry 260 people. Ferris didn't live long to enjoy his wheel's ongoing popularity. He died at age thirty-seven, just three years after creating the first one.

FAST FACT

What a Doll

Harold Matson and Elliot Handler started a toy-making enterprise in 1945, operating out of a California garage. For the name of their new company, they combined the first three letters of Matson's last name with the first two of Elliot's first name, added another *t*, and came up with Mattel.

Meanwhile, Elliot's wife, Ruth, observed their young daughter playing with baby dolls. The daughter liked to pretend the dolls were grown ups, imagining them in teenage or career-women roles.

Ruth became convinced there should be a doll that would inspire little girls to think about what they wanted to be when they were older. She set about to design a doll that wasn't a baby. (As Ruth said, "The doll should have breasts.")

Matson had already sold his half share of Mattel to the Handlers when Elliot and Ruth introduced their new doll at the 1959 New York Toy Fair.

The Handlers named the doll after their daughter Barbara, who inspired it. They always called her Barbie, so the doll became the Barbie Doll.

Since that 1959 introduction, more than one billion Barbies have been sold.

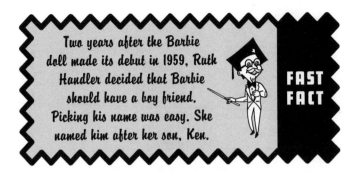

Two years after the Barbie doll made its debut in 1959, Ruth Handler decided that Barbie should have a boy friend. Picking his name was easy. She named him after her son, Ken.

FAST FACT

A Famous Symbol for Thirty-Five Bucks

The Nike swoosh has been called one of the most recognized symbols in the world. Nike doesn't even have to put their name on uniforms or ads. When the swoosh appears, people rarely mistake it.

Here's how they got that valuable symbol for the amazing price of $35.

Shortly after track runner Phil Knight and his coach, Bill Bowerman, started Nike in the 1960s, Phil was supplementing his meager Nike income by teaching accounting at Portland State University. There, he asked a graphic design student, Carolyn Davidson, if she would draw a logo for his new company. She agreed.

In a few days, Carolyn gave a design to Phil—with an invoice for $35. Phil had his logo, and Carolyn was happy to pocket $35 for a couple hours' work.

That's not quite the end of the story. In 1983, after Nike had attained undreamed of success and their swoosh had become world famous, Carolyn was invited to Nike's offices. When she arrived she was given two gifts: a swoosh ring embedded with a diamond, and an envelope containing an undisclosed amount of Nike stock. The $35 logo had paid off for everybody.

Starting on the Cheap

Not only did Nike get its renowned logo for $35, but the whole company was founded with just $1,000. Phil Knight and Bill Bowerman each kicked in $500 and began selling foreign athletic shoes at high school and college track meets on the West Coast.

Bowerman, the track coach at the University of Oregon, and Knight, one of his runners, had become convinced that lighter foreign sneakers were superior to what most Americans were wearing then.

After some success selling their imported shoes, Phil and Bill began manufacturing their own—and making improvements. One morning Bowerman was using a waffle iron at home. As he looked at it, he got the idea of a deep waffle-shaped pattern on the soles of their shoes for better traction. It was a success, and became a world standard for sneakers.

The company that was started on the cheap grew to annual sales of more than $8 billion.

Originally called Blue Ribbon Sports, Nike was later given the name of the Greek goddess of victory.

FAST FACT

Work Hard, Play Hard

Working for the U.S. Navy in 1943, Richard James, a marine engineer, was experimenting with springs that would keep ship instruments from gyrating with the sea's movement.

One day, a set of his coiled springs fell off a shelf. It didn't just fall to the floor, but seemed to climb down to lower shelves, and then, when it reached the floor, it took a step.

James was intrigued. He took the spring to a stairway and found it could descend the stairs by itself.

That convinced him he had discovered a new toy.

James's wife, Betty, went through a dictionary for several days trying to find just the right word to describe the spring's movements. She came up with *slinky*.

Betty and Richard trademarked the name Slinky (with a capital *S*) and began to manufacture and market the toy in 1946.

It became a successful family business operating out of Holidaysburg, Pennsylvania, where millions of Slinkys have been made since.

FAST FACT

A man named Adi Dassler took his first name and combined it with the first three letters of his last name to create the moniker for his brand of shoes: Adidas.

Word Game Inventor Was a Bad Speller

Odd as it seems, the man who created Scrabble, Alfred Butts, was himself a bad speller. His wife, Nina, helped him with the spelling part as he was conceiving his word game.

Alfred fooled around with the creation of Scrabble for years. He started working on it at his home in Newton, Connecticut, in 1931. He painted wooden tiles, each with a letter of the alphabet, then kept trying to figure out the best point value for each letter based on frequency of use.

He went through several name changes for his game. He originally called it Lexiko, then Criss Cross, and finally, Scrabble.

At last, in 1948—seventeen years after he began—Alfred was ready to copyright the name and rules. He took it to game manufacturer Selchow & Righter and they agreed to put it on the market.

For the man who couldn't spell so well, his invention became the best-selling word game in the world, and the second-best board game in sales, after Monopoly.

> Arthur Wynn, the man who invented crossword puzzles, originally called them "wordcross" puzzles but a printing error accidentally transposed the words and created "crossword." Since "crossword" appeared as the title of the puzzle on its first day in the newspaper, that's the name that stuck.
>
> **FAST FACT**

The Sound Behind the Name

All Japanese words end in a vowel or the letters *y* or *n*. Thus, we have such Japanese brand names as Toyota, Honda, and Nissan; such Japanese cities as Tokyo, Osaka, and Kyoto; and such personal names as those of the two men who founded Sony, Morita Akio and Ibuka Masaru.

When Akio and Masaru started their company after World War II, their aim was to use new technology developed during the war and apply it to consumer electronic products.

Their company was originally called Tokyo Tsushin Kogyo, but they realized as business expanded worldwide, they needed a brand name that was shorter and easier to pronounce.

Aiko searched dictionaries in different languages and came up with *sonus*, the Latin word for sound. Sonus, however, wouldn't work in the Japanese language, so needing a vowel sound or an *n* to end the word, Aiko changed Sonus to Sony.

FAST FACT The first Barbie dolls sold for $3. Today, those original dolls fetch as much as $10,000 at auctions.

A Spot to Drink

Big Thanks
to the Bookkeeper

In 1886, John Pemberton, a pharmacist in Atlanta, Georgia, invented a new soft drink. Unfortunately he had no idea what to call his invention. One day he was discussing the dilemma with his bookkeeper, Frank Robinson.

Robinson, who had no experience in advertising or marketing, almost off-handedly came up with what many experts say is now the most recognized brand name on earth.

Robinson looked at two of the ingredients in Pemberton's beverage and suggested *coca* from the coca leaves and *kola* from the kola nuts. To make both words start with the same letter, Robinson changed *kola* to *cola*—thereby creating not only the famous trademark, Coca-Cola, but also inventing the generic word *cola*, adapted by many soft drinks to follow.

As if that historic contribution wasn't enough, Robinson's own handwriting can be found in the distinctive, flowing script the brand Coca-Cola still uses today.

Let's hope this bookkeeper received some much-deserved overtime pay!

A Soda But No Smile

Think you've suffered bad luck? Let's revisit John Pemberton. He invented what would become the No. 1 soft drink in the world.

(Yeah, you're surely wrecked with sympathy. It's rough starting a multi-billion-dollar empire!)

But as fate would have it, Pemberton's role was short-lived—literally.

Pemberton was in debt and in poor health when he created Coca-Cola in 1886. He died just two years later, allowing another Atlanta druggist, Asa Candler, to buy complete ownership of Coca-Cola—its formula, its name, everything—for the grand total of $2,300.

That's right…$2,300.

Candler wisely gave up his drugstore to concentrate exclusively on Coke. Within nine years, the soda pop was sold in every state in the Union.

It was a huge success but its potential was still untapped. Originally Coca-Cola was sold only as a soda fountain drink. That would soon change.

Two men, Benjamin Thomas and Joseph Whitehead of Chattanooga, Tennessee, came to see Candler in 1900. They said they'd reveal two magic words with the stipulation that if Candler agreed with them, Thomas and Whitehead would share in Coca-Cola's success. Candler agreed.

The two words: Bottle it.

Soon after, Thomas and Whitehead became the first of Coke's bottlers across the country. The new distribution fueled the beverage's worldwide growth.

(Not a bad return on a $2,300 investment. Poor John Pemberton.)

Not the Ideal Nickname

As Coca-Cola became popular, people started referring to it as "Coke." The company wasn't so happy with the nickname and in fact never used it in ads or on the drink.

However, some nicknames become difficult to shake. The shorthand became so commonly used, the company had no choice but to accept it. "Coke" was registered as a trademark of Coca-Cola and today they proudly use *Coke* in advertisements and on their product.

Even Santa Claus Gets Thirsty

Everyone knows what Santa Claus looks like—the jolly, old man with a big belly, fur-trimmed red outfit, and unmistakable full, white beard. Along with Disney's Mickey Mouse, he's one of the most recognizable figures—real or fictitious—in the United States.

As hard as it is to imagine, dear Old St. Nick didn't always have the ruddy, rotund appearance we associate with him today. For many years, Santa Claus was depicted as everything from a tall, thin man to a small elf. And sometimes the twinkle in his eyes was replaced with a stern look. Even his outfit has changed—ranging from a bishop's robe to coats of different colors.

But in the early 1930s, all that changed when Coca-Cola began using drawings of Santa drinking a Coke in their magazine ads. The artist hired by Coke, Haddon Sundblom, gave Santa the distinctive red outfit we now know so well, and portrayed him as a chubby, joyful man of average size with a thick, white beard.

That particular image of Santa was then increasingly copied by Christmas card makers, retail merchants, and others. Together Coke and Sundblom created our modern image of Santa Claus.

Actually, pictures of Sundblom show that he might have served as his own source of inspiration: The bearded artist looked very much like today's Santa.

The Commercial That Climbed the Charts

In 1971 Coca-Cola began running a new TV and radio commercial. The upbeat commercial included a catchy song with these lyrics:

> I'd like to teach the world to sing,
> in perfect harmony
> I'd like to buy the world a Coke,
> and keep it company.

Well, the world not only wanted to sip, it also wanted to sing along. Thousands of people flooded media stations with calls saying they wanted to hear the commercial again. It was a marketing and cultural hit on an unprecedented and unanticipated scale.

Coca-Cola was fast to respond to the ad's popularity. Since the song was originally recorded by a group of multi-national singers on a hillside in Italy, Coca-Cola called the group the Hillside Singers. As the commercial gained in popularity, its single was re-recorded by a professional group, the New Seekers, and reached the Top 10 on the pop music charts.

Years before MTV, Coca-Cola unwittingly created one of the first "music videos." And unlike any brand—before or since—it spawned a true *commercial* hit.

Brad's Drink?
You Know It by Another Name

Four years after pharmacist John Pemberton of Atlanta invented Coca-Cola in 1886, another pharmacist was inspired to create a soft drink of his own to serve customers at his drugstore's soda fountain in New Bern, North Carolina. His name was Caleb Bradham—known around town as Brad—so he called his new beverage "Brad's Drink."

Never heard of it?

People in New Bern seemed to like the drink, leading Brad to run some newspaper ads to promote it in nearby towns. In the ads, Bradham described Brad's Drink as exhilarating, invigorating, and full of pep.

Getting warmer?

The more Brad thought about that word *pep*, the more he liked it.

On August 28, 1898, he officially changed the name of Brad's Drink to…Pepsi-Cola.

Thus, within the space of a few years, two Southern pharmacists had created new beverages that would become two of the most popular—and competitive—drink brands in the world.

Invigorating indeed.

Brad's New Lease on Life

For a while, sales of Brad's Drink under its new Pepsi-Cola name did well. Founder Caleb Bradham opened distribution centers around North Carolina and beyond.

But the cost of rapid expansion, plus competition from Coca-Cola, took its toll. Pepsi began to fall on hard times, running far behind Coke.

Disheartened, Brad lost control of the company. By 1923 Pepsi-Cola was bankrupt.

In bankruptcy court, a group of businessmen bought the company's assets for $30,000 and then tried to resume the fight for supremacy with Coke. But Pepsi still trailed its competitor by a big margin—until a great idea surfaced in the 1930s.

In those days, Coke and other soft drinks were sold in six-ounce bottles at five cents a pop (pun intended). Pepsi came out with a twelve-ounce bottle for the same five cents—doubling the refreshment—and advertised it in a milestone radio commercial.

That commercial not only dramatically increased Pepsi's sales, it brought broadcasting and advertising to a whole new level.

A Commercial Milestone

One incredibly successful advertising campaign can turn a company around. Such was the case with Pepsi-Cola.

You already know that in the late 1930s, Pepsi wanted to set themselves apart from the competition, and thus offered a twelve-ounce bottle of beverage for just a nickel. But the question was how best to promote this difference to the consumers.

The genius answer was to create an entirely new way of broadcast advertising—a musical jingle. Advertising jingles soon became commonplace, but Pepsi had the first famous one and placed it on radio stations throughout the country. It was played so often, millions of people learned the lyrics by heart.

There are some folks of a certain age today who can still recall Pepsi's legendary words:

"Pepsi-Cola hits the spot,
Twelve full ounces, that's a lot,
Twice as much for a nickel, too,
Pepsi-Cola is the drink for you.
Nickel, nickel, nickel, nickel."

That revolutionary commercial and its infectious jingle put Pepsi back in the major leagues of soft drinks.

Is There a Doctor in the House?

Yes, there was a real Dr. Pepper—but he didn't invent the drink named after him.

Dr. Charles Pepper owned a drug store in Rural Retreat, Virginia. One of his employees was a young man named Charles Alderton who liked to experiment concocting different-flavored drinks.

In 1885, Alderton left Dr. Pepper's store and moved to Waco, Texas, where he took a job at Morrison's Old Corner Drug Store. It was there that Alderton perfected the formula for a new drink that was to become a national brand.

How then do we drink Dr. Pepper instead of Mr. Alderton?

Legend has it that Alderton was in love with Dr. Pepper's daughter and often talked about her and the doctor to customers in Waco. It was the Texas customers who suggested to Alderton that he name the drink after the Virginia doctor.

(There's no word as to whether Dr. Pepper's daughter was flattered or not.)

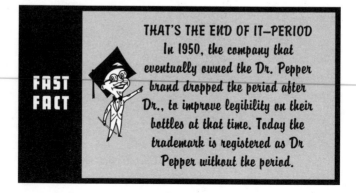

FAST FACT

THAT'S THE END OF IT—PERIOD
In 1950, the company that eventually owned the Dr. Pepper brand dropped the period after Dr., to improve legibility on their bottles at that time. Today the trademark is registered as Dr Pepper without the period.

WHAT'S WITH THE 10, 2, AND 4?
Ever notice those random numbers on the Dr Pepper bottle? They're not so random after all... Dr Pepper claims that research shows people's energy levels drop between meals at 10 a.m., 2 p.m., and 4 p.m. What better way to restore energy, they say, than to drink their pepper-upper at those times? To keep the competition at bay, the company registered the "10, 2 and 4" as part of their trademark.

FAST FACT

You Want Me to Drink WHAT?!

Charles Grigg of St. Louis spent much of the 1920s trying to develop a new soft drink. He experimented with eleven different formulas over the years before finally finding one he liked.

Its introduction to America in 1929 could have been better. Grigg brought out his drink just two weeks before the October 29 stock market crash that ushered in the Great Depression. Not the ideal time for a new product launch.

It might also have helped if Grigg had chosen a better name for his beverage.

He called it Bib-Label Lithiated Lemon-Lime Soda.

Not exactly catchy.

The tongue-twister was derived from one of the drink's original ingredients: lithium salts.

(How…refreshing.)

After a few years, the unwieldy name was wisely changed.

You now know this drink as 7 UP.

The 7 stands for the seven natural flavors blended into it. *UP* is for the bubbles in its carbonation.

(The company's marketing team has been thanking Grigg's decision ever since.)

FAST FACT The first soft drink company to come out with a so-called diet drink was Royal Crown Cola, in 1961. Their pioneering beverage was called Diet Rite.

Football's Favorite Drink

Practicing and playing under the hot Florida sun, members of the University of Florida's football team welcomed a refreshing new drink developed by doctors at their medical school.

The drink was originally designed to help Florida's athletes combat dehydration better than water alone.

It was 1965 when the beverage was officially introduced. Naming it was no problem. University of Florida teams are known as the Gators—so the new drink was called Gatorade.

Soon, hundreds of other sports teams—high school, college, and pro—began giving Gatorade to their players. Florida's edge became available to all athletes.

The drink and its logo can now be seen on the sidelines of football games everywhere, and after a big victory it's often used for a purpose that its creators probably never envisioned—it is ceremoniously dumped by players on their coaches.

A Family That Works Together, Stays Together

Beer giant Anheuser-Busch has been run continuously by the same single family longer than any other major American corporation.

The legacy began in 1857, when Adolphus Busch came to St. Louis, Missouri, from Kastel, Germany. Four years later, he married Lily Anheuser, whose father, Eberhard, owned a brewery.

The brewery was called Anheuser, but Eberhard Anheuser welcomed his new son-in-law by offering him a job and adding his name to the company, creating the Anheuser-Busch Brewing Co.

Soon, hard-working Adolphus Busch was named president, beginning the long string of Busch family members who've led the biggest beer-maker in the world. Adolphus and Lily Busch had thirteen children, ensuring generations of Busch leadership, up to the twenty-first century's August Busch III, who is currently president of Anheuser-Busch.

In the Busch family, it appears beer runs as thick as blood.

> *Anheuser-Busch's most famous product brand, Budweiser, is named after the town of Budweis, Czechoslovakia, where Adolphus Busch spent time as a child.*
>
> **FAST FACT**

In the Name of Love

German immigrant Jacob Best and his four sons opened a brewery in Milwaukee in 1844. For twenty years they used their family name and produced Best Beer, but a romance came along that changed everything.

One of Jacob's sons, Phillip, had a daughter Maria who fell in love with a Great Lakes steamship captain, Frederick Pabst. They married and Pabst bought half-interest in the brewery in 1864, when it was producing just 5,000 barrels a year. Nine years later, the output was 100,000 barrels, and Captain Pabst was not only named president of the company, but his name was put on the bottles.

The company came up with a gimmick in 1882 that is still identifiable today. They created an insignia by tying blue silk ribbons around their bottles after winning a blue ribbon first prize in a competition. Thus the now-famous name, Pabst Blue Ribbon Beer.

Adolphus vs. Adolph

While Adolphus Busch was building Anheuser-Busch in its early days, another German immigrant with a similar first name—Adolph Coors—was starting what would become one of its main competitors, the Coors brewery.

After working in a German brewery as a teenager to support himself following the deaths of both his parents, Adolph Coors came to America at age twenty-one. He dreamed of opening his own brewery. He worked his way west to raise money, and by age twenty-six, in 1873, had settled in Golden, Colorado, where he founded Coors Beer.

Today, more than 100 years later, Adolph and Adolphus's companies continue to battle it out for their share of the beer market. And just as Adolphus' descendents have continued to run his beer company, so have Adolph's. As of 2004, Coors is headed by fourth-generation Peter Coors.

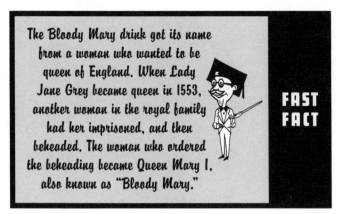

The Bloody Mary drink got its name from a woman who wanted to be queen of England. When Lady Jane Grey became queen in 1553, another woman in the royal family had her imprisoned, and then beheaded. The woman who ordered the beheading became Queen Mary I, also known as "Bloody Mary."

FAST FACT

It Happened Again

It's amazing how similar the origins are of today's top beer makers in America.

Each was founded at about the same time more than 100 years ago by a German immigrant, and each was run for many years by members of the founding family. It happened with Anheuser-Busch, Coors, and Miller Beer.

Frederick Miller left Germany in 1855, came to America, settled in Milwaukee, and bought a small brewery there for $9,000. Thus was born Miller Beer.

Frederick died in 1888, but family members continued to manage the business.

Way back in 1903, they came up with their famous, long-lasting slogan, "Miller High Life."

Miller achieved a milestone in beer making in 1969, with the introduction of a low-calorie beer, Miller Lite. The founders of Anheuser-Busch, Coors, and Miller would likely have approved because it helped sell more beer.

A Winning Loser

Sir Thomas Lipton was a Scottish competitive yachtsman. Unfortunately his passion for sailing didn't translate into victories at sea. In fact, Lipton lost millions of dollars over five futile attempts to win the America's Cup, the highest achievement in the expensive world of international yachting competition.

However, each time Lipton's yachts lost between 1899 and 1930, he showed such genuine, classic sportsmanship that he became a popular, sympathetic figure.

That was good for business.

You see, Lipton was also a tea merchant and one of the first savvy businessmen to recognize the importance of a brand name. Each time he prepared for and entered the yacht races, there was extensive press coverage. The resulting publicity helped make his name—and his brand of tea—well known. The good loser was a winner.

Lipton Tea became a top seller in America and elsewhere.

Everyone loves an underdog.

The U.S. President Who Created a Slogan

Nashville, Tennessee, was home to one of the great hotels in the South, where the rich and famous came to enjoy its hospitality, its food—and its special blend of coffee.

The hotel was named the Maxwell House.

One day in the early 1900s, President Theodore Roosevelt visited the Maxwell House and was served their special coffee. After finishing it, he was asked if he would like another cup. Reportedly Roosevelt replied, "Will I have another? Delighted! It's good to the last drop."

When the Maxwell House brand went national, they used Roosevelt's "good to the last drop" as their slogan. It became one of the best-known and longest-lasting slogans of all time. (Still, some jokesters occasionally asked what was wrong with the last drop.)

The slogan, and Roosevelt's involvement in it, helped vault Maxwell House coffee into a top-selling brand.

Never underestimate a Presidential endorsement.

A Saltwater Solution

For years Dr. Ludwig Roselius of Germany searched for a way to decaffeinate potent coffee beans without removing their flavorful punch. He received his big break by way of a storm in 1903, when a shipload of coffee beans traveling from Europe to America became waterlogged en route. Roselius discovered that by roasting the saltwater-soaked beans, one could remove 97 percent of the coffee's caffeine without sacrificing its flavor.

A few years later, in 1906, Roselius patented the decaffeination process, and soon after he started a company called Kaffee Hag. In 1923 he brought the product to America as Sanka, creating the name from a contraction of the French phrase *sans caf-*

feine, or without caffeine. He took the "san" from sans and the "ka" from the sound of the first two letters of caffeine.

Sanka became the forerunner of many other decaf brands in the years to come. It wasn't until well after World War II, though, that decaf coffee gained widespread popularity due to its perceived advantage. Whereas regular coffee threatened to keep drinkers awake, Sanka promised—in an early slogan—that one could "Drink it and sleep."

Orange Juice Surprise

The modern process of making fresh-tasting orange juice available year-round was developed in Massachusetts, of all places, even though no orange trees grow in the state.

The National Research Corporation (NRC) of Boston had just invented a process of dehydrating and prolonging the life of penicillin and streptomycin when the U.S. Army issued an open order for 500,000 pounds of powdered orange juice for its troops in World War II.

NRC used the same technology they had developed for medicines to make powdered orange juice for the Army. At the end of the war they adapted it for a consumer product. NRC also began testing frozen orange juice concentrate, resulting in a famous orange juice brand.

From Boston, the city famous for its Minutemen in the Revolutionary War, the name "Minute Maid" seemed perfect for the innovative orange juice, reflecting both history and its quick convenience of preparation.

FAST FACT

A blind Benedictine monk was put in charge of vineyards at his monastery in 1664. The monk, Dom Perignon, couldn't see the grapes he grew, but he could taste — and he developed the drink we know today as champagne. Champagne got its name because the monastery was in the old province of Champagne in France. An elite brand of champagne was coined Dom Perignon, in honor of the industrious monk.

5

In the Kitchen and Around the House

Gell-O?

A man by the name of Pearle Wait was a carpenter and cough medicine manufacturer in the upstate New York town of LeRoy.

He and his wife, Mary, liked to experiment with creating foods, and one day in 1897, they took some gelatin, added fruit flavor, and invented what would later become a popular product. Whether intentionally or by accident, they misspelled *gelatin* and came up with the name Jell-O.

The funny thing is, Mary and Pearle didn't think their creation was worth very much. Two years later they sold it to a neighbor, Francis Woodward, a small-time cereal manufacturer, for $450.

Woodward soon stopped making cereal when sales of Jell-O took off.

Now owned by Kraft, Jell-O has been helped by innovative advertising over the years, including a ten-year sponsorship of the No. 1 radio program of the 1930s, *The Jack Benny Show*. Benny made Jell-O a national catch-word by opening the program each week by saying not, "Hello again everyone," but, "Jell-O again everyone."

Birdseye's Vision

Although it sounds like a made-up brand name, Birdseye frozen foods are named after a man whose last name really was Birdseye.

It was Clarence Birdseye who pioneered the development of packaged frozen foods.

Even cavemen knew you could preserve food by keeping it cold. They learned this trick by storing food in their cold caves. Freezing preserves food because it inhibits the chemical changes and growth of microorganisms that cause spoilage.

However, commercial sales of frozen food didn't become popular until the mid-1900s. Much of the frozen food before that was frozen too slowly, causing some or all of its flavor to be lost.

Enter Clarence Birdseye. On a fur-trading trip to Labrador, Canada, he discovered that quickly-frozen fish were still flavorful and fresh when thawed.

Back in his Massachusetts home, Birdseye invented a process of fast-freezing that protected food quality along with taste and texture. It was the beginning of an industry that now sells a near-endless variety of frozen food products, from peas to pies to pizza.

Bibb lettuce got its name from Major John Bibb of Kentucky, who developed it in the 1850s.

FAST FACT

Breakfast Breakthrough

Before the 1900s, if a family wanted to eat breakfast cereal, they had to prepare it themselves. But in the early part of the twentieth century, Will Kellogg revolutionized the breakfast food industry.

Kellogg ran a sanitarium in his hometown of Battle Creek, Michigan, and developed what he called a health food for his patients—ready-to-eat corn flakes.

The patients seemed to enjoy Will's corn flakes, so in 1906, he took to the road and began selling Kellogg's corn flakes and then other cereals around the country. Will was a master salesman and built the first great breakfast cereal company.

Meanwhile, one of the patients at the sanitarium was a man named C. W. Post. He latched onto the idea, developed grape nut flakes, and eventually created the Post Cereal Company.

Off the Farm

Margaret Rudkin, a mother of three young children, discovered that one of her sons had an allergy to commercial breads that contained certain preservatives and artificial ingredients.

So she began experimenting with baking her own preservative-free bread for her family and soon perfected a whole-wheat loaf that contained only natural ingredients. Friends and family liked the bread, and that led Margaret to start a small business out of her kitchen in 1937, making loaves to sell to local grocers.

What to call the bread? That was easy. She named it after her family farm in Fairfield, Connecticut. The farm was known for years as the Pepperidge Farm.

As part of that expanding brand, Margaret Rudkin also brought goldfish crackers to the U.S. in 1962, after getting the recipe on a trip to Switzerland.

What's with the Balloons?

Elmer Cline of the Taggart Baking Company in Indi-anapolis was getting ready to bring out a new brand of bread in 1921.

While thinking about what to call the bread, Cline visited an international balloon race that was being held that year at the Indianapolis Speedway.

As Cline viewed the hundreds of colorful balloons filling the air above the Speedway, he said to a friend, "What a wonder," then realized he had discovered a good name for his new bread.

To mark the moment, balloons are featured in Wonder's logo and packaging. Wonder Bread has continued to use red, blue, and yellow balloons on the wrappers of their loaves since 1921.

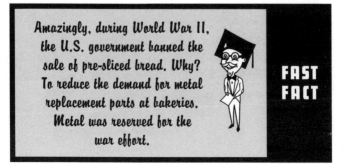

Amazingly, during World War II, the U.S. government banned the sale of pre-sliced bread. Why? To reduce the demand for metal replacement parts at bakeries. Metal was reserved for the war effort.

FAST FACT

They're Called English Muffins–But They're Not From England

Despite their name, people in England never heard of or saw English muffins until they were imported from the United States.

In the late l890s, Samuel Thomas baked the first English muffins—not in England, but in America—and created the Thomas' English Muffin brand.

Thomas got the idea from baking dough on griddles, which gave the muffins their distinctive "nooks and crannies" that hold gobs of butter and jam.

English muffins became an essential ingredient for an all-American creation, Eggs Benedict—a linguistic oddity that calls for *Canadian* bacon, *Hollandaise* sauce, and *English* muffins, but is very American.

Eggs Benedict was first made by a chef at New York's Waldorf-Astoria hotel shortly after English muffins were invented. The Waldorf chef made Eggs Benedict for, and named them after Sam Benedict, a businessman who was a good customer.

Not What You Think

Russian dressing is not from Russia. It was first made in America.

French fries are not from France. They were first made in Belgium.

Spaghetti originated not in Italy, but in China.

Chop suey and fortune cookies did not come from China, but were first made in the U.S.

Sauerkraut didn't begin in Germany but came from Chinese laborers building the Great Wall, who augmented their rice diet with fermented shredded cabbage.

Danish pastry, French toast, and Spanish rice were neither named nor popularized in Denmark, France, nor Spain, respectively, but in America.

On the other hand, the expression "As American as apple pie," does not ring true. Apple pie originated in France and England.

This Famous Brand Almost Didn't Make It

Six years after Henry John Heinz founded the H. J. Heinz Company, he and the company went bankrupt.

At Christmastime in 1875, Heinz was in such bad shape that he didn't have enough money to feed his family. Today Heinz food is on millions of tables, but at that dark point, Heinz couldn't provide enough food for his own.

Two months after filing for bankruptcy, Henry Heinz restarted his company. He got his brother, John, and a cousin, Frederick, to advance him $1,600. His wife received $400 from an inheritance, and Henry borrowed $1,000 from a neighbor.

With total capital equaling the princely sum of $3,000, Henry built what would become a global, billion-dollar enterprise.

FAST FACT

When the Ore-Ida frozen french fry brand started, they operated out of both Ontario, Oregon, and Burley, Idaho. So when it came time to pick a name, they combined the Ore from Oregon and the Ida from Idaho.

Two Brands with Same Product, Same Name

There were two unrelated families in Pittsburgh both named Heinz. And both started food companies called Heinz.

They sold the same products—like Heinz ketchup— and even used similar-looking labels to identify their foods.

Henry J. Heinz, who started his company first, was furious that someone else came along and was using his name. But the other Heinz family said, "You can't stop us. We're using our name just like you do."

Today such a thing would probably bring an unfair-business lawsuit, but this was in the 1880s and no suit was ever filed. However, things finally turned in Henry Heinz's favor.

The "other" Heinzes eventually couldn't pay their bank loans, and all their company assets were put up for sale. Henry went to the auction and bought everything—machinery, manufactured goods, containers—and put them on a barge. On Henry's orders the barge was towed to the middle of a river in front of his own plant and sunk.

It was said that H. J. Heinz literally sank his competition.

On what two days do Americans eat the most food? According to a survey by Hallmark Cards, the biggest day for food consumption in American homes is Thanksgiving. The day that ranks second is Super Bowl Sunday. (Pass the nachos.)

FAST FACT

What's in Those
Food Brands You Buy?

Surprisingly, until 1990 there was no federal law in the United States requiring that nutritional facts be displayed on food products. Today, however, you'll find a plethora of information listed on labels.

The law mandates the size of the nutritional panel and where it's to be placed. The panel must give you information on such things as calories, fat, cholesterol, protein, potassium, sodium, carbohydrates, vitamins, and percent of daily values.

And to prevent misleading consumers, there's a specific order to the list of ingredients that must be on packages and bottles of food. Ingredients are listed in descending order of quantity.

It's None of Your Business

A food company employee tells the story about a customer who wrote to a manufacturer, asking what ingredients were in a package of food she had just bought.

This was in the days before companies were required to list ingredients. The manufacturer directed that the customer be told, "It's none of your business what we put in our food." Such philosophy was not unusual when some food processors wanted to keep their ingredients secret, either for competitive reasons or unscrupulous ones, or both.

Cantaloupe got its name from the place where it was first grown—the papal summer residence of Cantalupo, Italy.

FAST FACT

No Kissing!

In 1910, Martin Bogdanovich bought a boat and set out to catch tuna fish off the coast of California.

Martin's simple beginning was the start of a gigantic operation. As he caught more and more tuna, he kept buying more boats and eventually formed a family company to process, package, and distribute the fish. But his tuna still had no brand name.

In the 1940s, when Bogdanovich's son Joe became president of the company, Joe began searching for a name. A food broker at the White Star brokerage firm suggested the word *Star* and said, "Why not have a kissing couple on the label and call the brand Star Kist?"

Joe liked the name, but not the kissing couple. The StarKist label, without the kissing couple, first appeared on tuna cans in 1942.

The company capitalized on the name "Star" by using Hollywood stars to endorse the tuna. It helped put StarKist on the national map.

Sorry, Charlie

The Charlie in this famous phrase was a cool fish who looked hip, but always got rejected.

He was created by Tom Rogers, an employee at the Leo Burnett advertising agency. Rogers modeled Charlie after a street character that he remembered from his teenage years in New York City. Rogers gave Charlie sunglasses and a cap and called him Charlie the Tuna. To give Charlie his classic New York accent, Rogers selected actor Herschel Bernardi.

Charlie made his debut appearance in TV ads for StarKist tuna in 1962. He's still hanging around.

Charlie always endeavors—in vain—to be selected (and presumably slaughtered) for a can of StarKist. Alas, the fishy fellow is rejected each time as not good enough, turned away with the solemn remark, "Sorry Charlie."

You often see the word "albacore" on cans of tuna. Albacore is the only species of tuna that has all white meat.

FAST FACT

Mrs. Fish

Edward Piszek and his partner founded a frozen seafood empire in 1946 by accident.

They ran a food concession for a Philadelphia tap-room, and Ed's specialty was making deviled crab cakes. One night he prepared 172 and sold only fifty. Instead of throwing the extra crab cakes away, he stuck them in a freezer that had just been installed. (Food freezers were a relatively new phenomenon in those days.)

When he reheated the frozen crab cakes a week later, customers liked them. Shortly thereafter Ed and his friend John Paul each anted up $350 to start a frozen seafood business.

Ed's mother wanted him to call the new company Mrs. Piszek's Kitchens, but the two partners took John's mother's name instead and called it Mrs. Paul's Kitchens. Before long, Mrs. Paul's fish sticks became well known, as did other Mrs. Paul's products. The name Mrs. Piszek's fish sticks never made it.

He Gave Birth to a Tiger, a Giant, a Fish, Elves, and a Doughboy

Leo Burnett ran an advertising agency in Chicago that became famous in the marketing industry for creating a menagerie of what Burnett called "critters:" life-like, loveable symbols for his clients' brands.

For Kellogg's cereals, Burnett's agency came up with Tony the Tiger; for Green Giant vegetables, the Jolly Green Giant; for StarKist tuna, Charlie the Tuna; for Keebler cookies and crackers, the Elves; and for Pillsbury baked goods, the Pillsbury doughboy.

Not bad work for one creative agency.

But things weren't always so easy for these beloved little brand mascots. Tony the Tiger almost didn't have a long life. When he was introduced, on Kellogg's Frosted Flakes, he was rotated with an elephant, a kangaroo, and a gnu character. Kellogg intended to eliminate three of the four animals eventually, and Tony was a candidate for the trash heap until Kellogg noticed that the boxes bearing the not-so-fearsome tiger outsold the rest.

(A relieved Tony was heard to say, "Gr-r-reat!")

Whence Came Wheaties?

Today, when new products hit the market, companies often employ focus groups and hire expensive experts to create a name.

But when General Mills's new wheat flakes were ready to be packaged for breakfast tables in 1924, a woman named Jane Bausman, the wife of a General Mills executive, tried the cereal and quickly said, "Why not call them Wheaties?"

It was as simple as that. One of the most famous brand names in the world was born.

The long-lasting Wheaties slogan, "Breakfast of Champions," came along in 1933 when the cereal began to feature sports stars on the boxes.

While Wheaties has never had a name change, another General Mills top seller, Cheerios, has gone through several. It was introduced in 1941 as Cheerioats. Then on packages it became two words, with *Cheeri* on one line and *oats* below it. In 1945, the company left out the oats part and the cereal was crowned *Cheerios*.

The Good, the Bad, and the Ugly

The folks at Hormel Foods get a little sick to their stomachs when they see what's happened to the name of their popular lunchmeat Spam.

Hormel introduced the word *Spam* when they launched the product in 1937. Since then they say they've sold more than six billion cans of the ham. In recent years they've watched with dismay as *spam* has commonly come to mean junk e-mail, a source of heartburn and anger for computer users.

How did the two spams get their names? Hormel had a contest to name their lunchmeat and entrant Kenneth Daigneau won $100 for suggesting *Spam*; he combined the first two letters of *spiced* and the last two of *ham*.

For junk e-mail, early Internet users originally employed the word in tribute to a popular skit by the Monty Python comedy group. In the skit, a woman tries to order breakfast in a cafe that serves Spam with every order. She keeps telling the waitress she doesn't want any Spam. A group at the next table begins chanting, "Spam, Spam" louder and louder, drowning out other conversations. The skit apparently left an impression on computer geeks. So when unwanted e-mails began to appear in large numbers, they dubbed them *Spam*.

Perhaps the most misnamed product of all time is the beloved hamburger. The unassuming patty of ground beef has absolutely nothing to do with ham. The food got its name from its city of origin, Hamburg, Germany.

FAST FACT

The Little Girl with the Umbrella

Few advertising slogans and symbols have lasted as long—or been more memorable—than the one used by Morton Salt.

In 1911, Morton developed a way to make their salt flow easily even in damp weather. They asked their advertising agency to come up with a campaign to promote this new advance.

The agency created a picture of a little girl under an umbrella, and used the words of an old proverb: "When it rains, it pours." The ad first appeared in *Good Housekeeping* magazine in 1914.

Morton has been using that symbol and slogan ever since, although they have updated the hairstyle and dress on the girl. They've changed her looks on the average of once every ten years.

FAST FACT

Chicken à la king was named after a real king. King Edward VII of England in the early 1900s loved the dish and had it specially prepared for himself.

With a Name Like This . . .

If you were picking a good brand name for your products, you probably wouldn't choose the somewhat funny-sounding Smuckers. However, the J. M.

Smucker Company was sort of stuck with that name since it was their founder's last name, and he used it on their products.

The company's founder was Jerome Monroe Smucker of Orrville, Ohio. Mr. Smucker began the business by making apple cider and apple butter in 1897, then selling his wares around the Orrville area from the back of a horse-drawn wagon.

On each package he signed his name, creating the J.M. Smucker brand that became well known in eastern Ohio. In the 1920s, Smucker added jellies and then peanut butter to his line, and the company eventually went national in 1942.

The company made the most of its name with humor. They came up with the now-famous slogan: "With a name like Smuckers, it has to be good." That slogan was coined in 1962 and has been used ever since.

Say "Uncle"!

There was a rice grower in Texas who became something of a local legend for producing quality yields of his rice.

The rice grower was an African-American farmer known as Uncle Ben, and he achieved fame in his area when people began saying that a particularly good crop of rice was "as good as Uncle Ben's."

Meantime, the Gordon Harwell Company was marketing a brand called Harwell's Converted Rice. They decided it was time to change their name. Harwell chose to honor Uncle Ben by calling his company Uncle Ben's Inc., and its brand Uncle Ben's Rice. The company further honors Uncle Ben by depicting his portrait on its packaging.

Lois DeDomenico Stirs Up a New Dish

Four brothers—Vince, Paskey, Anthony, and Tom DeDomenico—owned the Golden Grain Macaroni Company of San Francisco.

One day in the 1950s, Tom's wife, Lois, got the idea to mix some rice with the macaroni from her husband's company. She served the dish at dinner one night and it became a family favorite.

Lois's special dish needed an appropriate name based on its macaroni-and-rice combination. Brother-in-law Vince took the word *rice*, added the last five letters of *macaroni*, and came up with Rice-a-Roni. It was introduced to the public in 1958.

The product was helped by a memorable ad campaign using the catchy jingle, "Rice-a-Roni, the San Francisco treat." Over the years, the company has added a selection of other products with chicken, beef, pastas and vegetables to go along with Lois' original rice and macaroni.

French's NOT From France

It may seem odd, but the makers of French's mustard and other products carrying that brand felt compelled to explain their name in connection with the Iraq War.

When the war began in 2003, there was some criticism of France in the United States because of the country's political opposition to the U.S. military invasion of Iraq.

That's when the French's mustard folks went out of their way to tell the nation that their company— despite its name—had nothing to do with France. It was in fact founded in America by an American.

The founder, George J. French, began the company by selling mustard at the St. Louis World's Fair in 1904.

Headquartered in Rochester, New York, French branched out with other products as well. It was in Rochester in 1920 that French made a hot sauce that kicked off the buffalo wing fad in nearby Buffalo, New York, and helped turn them into an all-American craze.

FAST FACT

Both the Nestle and Ovaltine brands originated in Switzerland. Ovaltine was invented by a Swiss chemist, Dr. Hans Wander, in 1904. Nestle was founded by Henri Nestle, a Swiss pharmacist, in the 1860s.

Ketchup's Fishy Past

Many people think ketchup is an American invention that is, was, and always will be made with tomatoes.
Think again.
Ketchup actually originated in China, where it was made from spiced fish (yes, fish), not tomatoes. More than 300 years ago, the Chinese called their tangy sauce *ketsiap*.

Shortly thereafter, ketsiap's popularity spread to the Malay Peninsula, where the Malaysians named it *kechap*.

Early in the eighteenth century, British sailors discovered the condiment and brought samples back to England, where people began to make it with tomatoes. The sauce was widely used throughout England, and English colonists ultimately brought it to America.

But the English didn't leave well enough alone. For some unknown reason they misspelled the sauce Malaysians had called kechap, adding a *t* and replacing the *a* with a *u*. The result? America's favorite condiment—*ketchup*.

Not all manufacturers were pleased with the spelling of the Asian-derived word ketchup, so they Anglicized it further, making it catsup. Other variations over the years have included katsup and catchup. A magazine writer once remarked, "Here's a sauce that everybody knows what it is, but nobody can spell it."

FAST FACT

The Lucky Number

Although Heinz's "57 Varieties" is one of the most famous and enduring business slogans, the number 57 was not and is not the number of products Heinz sells.

In fact, the number was chosen out of pure superstition.

The story begins when the company's founder, Henry J. Heinz, was riding an elevated train in New York City in 1896. He looked up and saw a car-card advertising twenty-one styles of shoes. He quickly decided to use that type of slogan for his own company.

At the time Heinz was manufacturing more than sixty products—but he thought fifty-seven was a magic, lucky number. According to his diary, the number fifty-seven kept turning in his mind, and so he came up with "57 Varieties." He was so taken with the number that as soon as he got back to his office in Pittsburgh, he began laying out plans to use "57" in all advertising.

Within a week "57 Varieties" was appearing in newspapers, on billboards, signboards, and, according to Heinz's dairy, "Everywhere else I could find a place to stick it."

Today, Heinz produces more than 5,700 varieties, but they still use the their famous "57."

The Amazing Advertisement of a Brand

No one has ever run a bigger, longer-lasting advertisement than Henry Heinz did for his Heinz "57" products.

In a grand gesture, Henry bought an ocean pier in Atlantic City, New Jersey. And it wasn't just your average pier. It was *huge*, extending the length of three football fields out into the Atlantic Ocean.

The pier was so big it contained a long boardwalk, a lounge, a reading room, a theater, a sun deck, an organ, an art pavilion, and an exhibit hall. It was free to the public and, of course, included displays of Heinz products and free food samples. Over the years, millions of people visited the Heinz Ocean Pier.

Attached to the roof was a seventy-foot-high electric sign with a large "57" that glowed each night and could be seen for miles.

The gigantic advertisement lasted for forty-six years—until a hurricane in 1944 destroyed it.

Not Your Average Frank

Harry Stevens was the concessionaire at a Major League baseball park in New York City in the early 1900s. One cool day, Harry wasn't selling much cold food, which was all that was served at games back then.

Harry went shopping for something warm to sell, and a neighborhood butcher offered to cook some sausages for him. But that posed another problem: How could fans at the game hold the sausages?

The answer was found at a neighboring bakery. Uniting sausages and bun, the hot dog was born.

But it didn't have a name yet.

A well-known sports cartoonist, Tad Dorgan, was at the same ballgame. Dorgan—after sampling the new food combination—drew a cartoon for the next day's newspaper. The shape of the sausages reminded him of a dachshund, so he portrayed the curious new item as a dachshund in a bun. Dorgan wanted to title the cartoon "Hot Dachshund," but he had trouble with its spelling. So he settled for "Hot Dog" and gave us a new name.

Dorgan's historic cartoon can still be seen at the Baseball Hall of Fame in Cooperstown, New York.

Where People Are Called Wieners

Wieners and frankfurters are common names for hot dogs—just don't order a wiener in Vienna, Austria.

Vienna's native German name is Wien—and its citizens are called Wieners. There's even a magazine in Vienna called *Wiener* magazine, but it's about life in Vienna, not hot dogs. No one would go to a butcher shop in Vienna and order a couple of wieners.

So what's the hot dog connection with Vienna?

Well, the reason Americans use the word wieners for hot dogs is because the savory sausages were first created in Vienna in 1789 by a local butcher, Johann Lahner. But he called them frankfurters after his original home, Frankfurt, Germany. They're still called frankfurters in Vienna.

Unlike the Viennese—or Wieners—those who live in Frankfurt, Germany, have no problem calling frankfurters, frankfurters.

There, the people and the food product happily co-exist with the same name.

(Perhaps in Frankfurt, you really *are* what you eat.)

Worcester . . . what?!

Sir Marcus Sandys, a British nobleman, became governor of a province in India in the mid-1800s.

While there, he acquired the recipe for a tangy sauce made from a secret blend of spices and seasonings.

When he returned to his estate in England, located in the town of Worcester, Sandys had bottles of the sauce prepared for his private use and as gifts for friends.

Its popularity prompted Sandys to license manufacturers to make the sauce commercially. It was named Worcester Sauce, in honor of his hometown.

But when the product debuted in America, its name was changed to Worcestershire, the word *shire* being the British equivalent of *county*.

Americans found it easy to enjoy the sauce, though perhaps not so much its pronunciation and spelling.

Put Some Mayo on That Sandwich

Everyone knows what mayonnaise is made from—eggs and oil.

But why do we call it mayonnaise? And where did it come from?

Originally, Spain.

Mayonnaise was first created on the Spanish island of Minorca in the Mediterranean Sea. The major port of Minorca is Mahon, which became famous in Europe for its delicious sauce, then simply called *Mahon* sauce.

French tourists brought the Mahon sauce recipe back to France. Chefs there used it for their best meats and renamed it *mahonnaise.*

When the spread eventually spread to the rest of Europe and America in the early 1800s, it was considered a delicate French creation, its Spanish origins forgotten.

The sauce's popularity grew as it was used on all kinds of food, and the English-speaking world changed its spelling, substituting a *y* for the *h* and making the formerly exotic *mahonnaise* today's ordinary *mayonnaise.*

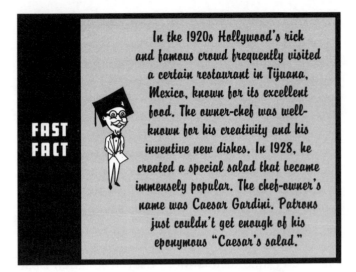

FAST FACT

In the 1920s Hollywood's rich and famous crowd frequently visited a certain restaurant in Tijuana, Mexico, known for its excellent food. The owner-chef was well-known for his creativity and his inventive new dishes. In 1928, he created a special salad that became immensely popular. The chef-owner's name was Caesar Gardini. Patrons just couldn't get enough of his eponymous "Caesar's salad."

The Six-Foot-Tall Microwave

Microwave ovens made their debut after World War II. The first commercial microwave models were produced by the Raytheon company in 1947. They were bigger than a refrigerator, weighed more than 700 pounds, and sold for several thousand dollars.

Not exactly something you'd find in the average kitchen.

The first microwaves weren't even made for homes, but for restaurants. Some tried the new-fangled machines and advertised the technology as Radar Ranges and Atom Cooking.

Fearing the food might be subject to undesired radiation, some people were wary of the microwave method. But anxiety gradually dissipated over the years when no ill effects were reported from microwave cooking.

The first home microwave model appeared in the mid-1950s. Made by Tappan, they were still rather bulky and very expensive. But in the ensuing years manufacturers learned how to reduce the size—and cost—of the units. Ultimately the former six-foot giants got much smaller and became more common, beginning a revolution in the way people prepare everyday food.

Dishes in Distress

Contrary to popular opinion, the international distress call for ships at sea—S.O.S.—does not stand for "Save Our Ship" or any other words. S.O.S. was chosen because it can be sent quickly and easily by Morse Code: three dots, three dashes, three dots.

However, S.O.S cleaning pads do stand for three words.

The story begins in 1917, when door-to-door salesman Edwin Cox of San Francisco was looking to boost the sales of his aluminum cookware. He kept hearing women complain about how food stuck to pans when they were cleaning. Inspired by this widespread kitchen predicament, Cox got the idea of combining the abrasiveness of steel wool with the cleaning ability of soap.

In his own kitchen he began to make little steel wool pads saturated with soap. He found a ready market for them. So good was the demand for his pads that Cox gave up his day job of selling pots and pans and set up the soap-pad business.

Cox's wife, erroneously thinking, as many people did, that the S.O.S. distress call stood for "Save Our Ship" or "Save Our Souls," suggested S.O.S for "Save Our Saucepans"—and that became their brand name.

FAST FACT

What's a maytag?
The Maytag Company was founded in 1893 by a man named F. L. Maytag of Newton, Iowa. Originally a farm equipment manufacturer, Maytag added its now famous washing machines to the lineup in the early 1900s.

That Arm and Hammer

Dr. Austin Church and John Dwight formed a company in 1846—a company still called Church & Dwight into the 2000s—but their famous brand name didn't come along until Dr. Church' s son James joined the firm in 1867.

James was a student of Roman mythology. He especially liked the story of Vulcan, the Roman god of fire who was skilled in making ornaments and weapons for other gods. James Church had a drawing made of Vulcan's arm holding a hammer, about to strike an anvil.

James's interest in Roman mythology created one of the longest-lasting brand names in America, Arm & Hammer. The brand was first used on Church & Dwight's baking soda, but it's now also used on a variety of their deodorizers, cleaners, pet care, oral care, and laundry products.

A Mysterious Symbol

In the grocery store, you may have noticed that many food product labels have a small circle with the letter *U* inside. What does that symbol actually mean?

It means the food is kosher, or suitable to eat for those who adhere to a kosher diet. The *U* stands for the Union of Orthodox Jewish Congregations, and it is their kosher seal of approval. Only products endorsed by the Union are permitted to carry the seal. To earn the seal, factory procedures have to be inspected by rabbis to make sure strict start-up and cleanup rules are followed.

Heinz's vegetarian beans became the first national brand to carry the "Circle U" in 1923.

Today, nearly 80,000 products in forty-eight countries display the "Circle U" near their brand name.

Unlikely Revolutionaries

One of the strangest revolutions in history ultimately gave the United States its fiftieth state and facilitated the emergence of a famous food brand.

Hawaii was an independent monarchy in the 1800s, known as the Kingdom of Hawaii. But in 1893, a bunch of upstarts changed all that.

The revolutionaries were businessmen—pineapple growers and sugar planters—who led a bloodless coup against the reigning Queen Liliuokalani. They removed her from the throne and established the

Republic of Hawaii with Sanford Dole as their new president.

The United States sent marines and naval officers to keep the peace, and in 1898, the U.S. annexed Hawaii as a territory. Sixty-six years later, in 1959, Hawaii officially became a state.

What about those revolutionaries? Sanford Dole, who became president, and later, governor, of Hawaii, came from a family that founded the pineapple business in Hawaii. His cousin, James Dole, became head of Dole Foods, a brand well known worldwide not only for pineapples but other fruits and vegetables as well.

The Janitor with the Lucky Connection

Murray Spangler spent years as an unsuccessful inventor, and the resulting debt forced him to take a job as a janitor in a department store in Canton, Ohio.

There, in 1908, still trying to invent something that would pay off, Spangler started fooling around with what would become the first practical, portable vacuum cleaner. He built a contraption made with a broom handle, a fan, a box, and a pillowcase. He called it a *suction sweeper*. He tested his invention at the department store and it worked wonders.

But his true good fortune came through a family connection. Spangler's cousin was Susan Hoover, married to a wealthy leather-goods factory owner, William Hoover. Susan convinced her husband to patent and manufacture cousin Murray's contraption. The vacuum cleaner was very successful. Murray was paid well for his invention and happily left his janitor job behind.

You might say the only bad part for Murray was that William named the vacuum a Hoover instead of a Spangler.

Cambridge Cups?

You would think that a brand called Dixie Cups had come from the land of Dixie—but it didn't.

While attending Harvard University in Cambridge, Massachusetts, in 1908, Hugh Moore got the idea for a sanitary, disposable paper cup and formed a business with the not-so-exciting name of Individual Drinking Cup Company.

Moore and his partner, Lawrence Luellen, called their product the Health Kup. After several years of financial struggle, they moved their headquarters south. However, they only went as far south as New York City, where they hoped to obtain more financing.

They were able to stay in business, but results were still not what they hoped. By 1919, Moore finally became convinced that the name Health Kup sounded too clinical and was pushing away mainstream consumers.

By chance, another manufacturer in the lower Manhattan loft building where Health Kups were produced made Dixie Dolls. Moore thought about that name, decided it was catchy, and asked the owner if he minded Moore using *Dixie* for his product. The owner agreed, and Dixie Cups were born (on Yankee soil).

FAST FACT

Before the Civil War, it was customary for local banks to issue their own money. A bank in the New Orleans area (where there was a large French-speaking population) produced $10 bills with the word "Dix" on them, which means "ten" in French. People started referring to the bills as "dixies," and riverboat men from the North began saying they were heading downriver to pick up some dixies in Dixie Land. In time, the name Dixie came to be applied to all of the Deep South.

He Couldn't Afford a Secretary—So He Gave Us the Answering Machine

When Joseph Zimmerman opened an air conditioning and heating company in Milwaukee after graduating as an electrical engineer from Marquette University in 1935, he didn't have enough money to hire a secretary. So he began tinkering with an answering machine that could take his calls when he was out of the office.

Zimmerman invented the first widely used answering machine with a generally recognized name. He called it the Electronic Secretary—and it was an elaborate contraption that lifted the phone receiver off the hook and used a phonograph to record the message. After thirty seconds the recorder shut down and a hoist returned the receiver to the hook.

The Milwaukee Public Museum now houses the original Electronic Secretary, and the museum's curator, John Lundstom, calls it a "real Rube Goldberg machine."

Answering machines reached their optimum popularity in the 1970s and '80s, but began to disappear with the widespread availability of voice-mail systems that are built right into phone systems.

6

The Daily Grind

The Product that
Wouldn't Work Sticks Around

Dr. Spence Silver, a research scientist at the 3M Company, created a new adhesive in the 1960s. Unfortunately the adhesive didn't really work too well—it stuck to things, but didn't stick permanently. You could say it was an adhesive that wasn't really an adhesive.

In meeting after meeting with his colleagues, Dr. Silver kept asking if anyone could think of a use for this new semi-stick adhesive. Nobody could help the good doctor.

Then serendipity entered the scene in, of all places, the choir loft of a church. There, another 3M employee, Art Fry, became frustrated when bookmarks kept falling out of his hymnal.

Fry had heard Dr. Silver wondering what to do with his pet adhesive. Eureka! The idea hit Fry one morning in church: Why not put Dr. Silver's adhesive on the back of little slips of paper that would stick to the page he wanted to mark, but then could be moved to another page for a later hymn?

You may have already guessed the result. In 1980, 3M introduced Post-It Notes.

What Came First?

You may be surprised to learn that facsimile transmission or faxing was invented *before* the telephone.

The ability to send written words and pictures over wires was first developed in 1843 by a Scottish clockmaker, Alexander Bain. His work evolved from Samuel Morse's invention of the telegraph seven years earlier.

The telephone wasn't invented until 1876.

While telephones quickly became popular, it wasn't till the 1970s and 1980s that fax machines were common. If the technology was there, why did it take more than 100 years for fax machines to take hold? One reason was that fax systems were originally more costly and complicated. Another was that manufacturers concentrated on other office products. It was not until 1966 that the first practical commercial fax machine was made, by Magnavox.

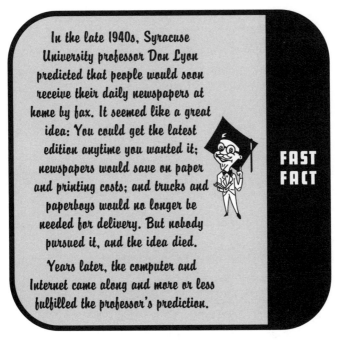

In the late 1940s, Syracuse University professor Don Lyon predicted that people would soon receive their daily newspapers at home by fax. It seemed like a great idea: You could get the latest edition anytime you wanted it; newspapers would save on paper and printing costs; and trucks and paperboys would no longer be needed for delivery. But nobody pursued it, and the idea died.

Years later, the computer and Internet came along and more or less fulfilled the professor's prediction.

FAST FACT

"Xerox It"

When people use a copy machine, they often say they are "Xeroxing." But they may well not be using a Xerox machine.

The Xerox brand name has become so popular it's used as a generic word for photocopying. However, the name is still the trademarked property of the Xerox Company alone.

Where did this odd name come from?

Chester Carlson, a physicist from Seattle, Washington, invented the process of what was called *xerography* in 1938. The *xero* (pronounced as if the *x* were a *z*) came from the Greek word for *dry* and the *graphy* stood for one of the definitions of *printing*.

Despite the trouble people originally had pronouncing and spelling Carlson's xerography, the invention revolutionized photocopying.

Carlson's invention, the basis for modern copiers, was acquired by the Haloid Company of Rochester, New York. Then, just as *facsimile* changed to *fax*, *xerography* morphed into *Xerox*. The copiers became so successful, the Haloid Company changed its own name to its product's name, and emerged as the present-day Xerox Corporation. (Copycat.)

A Tale of
Two Arthurs

Arthur Pitney and Arthur Bowes came together by accident. The chance meeting revolutionized mass mailing.

Until 1920 there was no such thing as metered mail for postal customers. All people, including those in business who made large mailings, had to lick each stamp on every envelope.

Pitney was an inventor who tinkered with various versions of a postage meter. The Post Office department took a look at his gadgets but rejected them.

On the scene appeared Bowes, who owned a company that sold stamp-canceling machines to the post office. He, too, had thought about a meter that could print postage. By chance, he heard through some postal employees about Pitney's attempts, and contacted him.

With Pitney's meter and Bowes' relationship with postal officials, they were able to get an exclusive license to print postage. The first piece of Pitney Bowes metered mail was posted on December 10, 1920.

It was a letter from Bowes to his wife.

A Broken Printer Ribbon Launches an Industry

On the July 4th weekend in 1985, grocery supermarket executive Tom Stemberg was writing a business plan for his stores when his printer ribbon broke. He went to find a new ribbon, but his local stationer was closed. He finally located one that was open, but they didn't have the correct ribbon in stock.

An idea hit Stemberg. Why not create a super-store for office supplies?

Ten months later, in May of 1986, Stemberg made his idea a reality. He opened his first office supply superstore in the Boston suburb of Brighton.

What to call his store? Stemberg took an ordinary product, capitalized its first letter, and used *Staples* as his brand name (the pun was probably intentional).

Staples grew into a chain that now boasts more than 1,500 stores throughout the U.S., Canada, and Europe. Competitor chains like Office Depot and Office Max followed. They sell staples, too (but with a small *s*).

Curly Haired Copy Center

At the start of a new school year in September 1970, Paul Orfalea borrowed money to open a photocopy shop near the campus of the University of California at Santa Barbara.

Just out of college himself, Paul's business idea was to provide photocopy service for students as well as a few school supplies, too.

With just one copying machine and a few display racks, the shop wasn't big. Paul ran that first shop as a one-man operation. Luckily, there was a taco restaurant next door; he drilled a hole in the wall so he could easily get a taco for lunch without leaving the store. Remarkably, it was the start of a chain that would eventually grow to over 1,200 branches around the world.

In college, Paul had earned a nickname based on his curly, red hair. He figured that nickname was as good as any for the name of his shop. His friends called him Kinko—and that was the beginning of Kinko's.

Scottish Tape?

A manufacturing error led to the creation of a famous brand name.

In 1925, Richard Drew of the 3M Company invented the first masking tape, designed to help auto painters make two-tone paint applications.

Drew tested a prototype roll with an auto painter in St. Paul, Minnesota. The painter applied the masking tape to the edge of the color already painted and was just about to spray on the second color when the tape fell off.

The annoyed painter examined the tape and saw it had adhesive only along its outer edges, but not in the middle. He said to Drew, "Take this tape back to those Scotch bosses of yours and tell them to put more adhesive on it."

Drew improved the tape, which still had no name. When he took the new version back to the painter, the painter asked if he was still trying to sell that "Scotch" tape. The name—like the tape—stuck.

In 1930, 3M brought out the first of its familiar see-through pressure-sensitive tapes, and decided to give all its varieties of tape the brand name of Scotch.

FAST FACT

The company that makes Post-It Notes and Scotch Tape began in 1902 in a Lake Superior town called Two Harbors, Minnesota. From Two Harbors it became 3M, which stood for Minnesota Mining & Manufacturing (the original business mined minerals to make sandpaper and other abrasives).

7

The Computer Age

Would You Have Bet on This Man?

He was a college dropout. He was so painfully shy that friends nearly had to drag him out of the house to socialize. He started a little company, but it struggled.

However, by age thirty-one he had become the youngest billionaire in U.S. history, and a few years later he was the richest man in America.

His name: Bill Gates. He called his little company Micro-soft (with a hyphen)—combining *Micro* from microcomputer and *soft* from software. He began writing computer programs and had a few clients, but then several went bankrupt and the future of Micro-soft looked glum.

In 1980, Gates got his first big break. IBM was making its first personal computers and Gates was able to license his operating system to them. After his company's early struggles, Gates dropped the hyphen, and created Microsoft.

By 1986 Microsoft went public and Gates was a billionaire.

FAST FACT

Two of Bill Gates's high school friends were Paul Allen and Steve Ballmer. Allen became Gates's partner in the early days of Microsoft and wound up as the third-richest man in America via his company stock. Ballmer, who used to drag the shy Gates to high school parties, was repaid when Gates named him president of Microsoft.

CTR Adopts a Much Better-Known Name

A company that made punch cards and electric accounting machines was incorporated in 1911 as Computing-Tabulating-Recording Company, or CTR.

You know them today by the name they switched to in 1924: the International Business Machines Company, or IBM.

IBM's major breakthrough as a giant corporation came in 1935, when the first Social Security Act was passed. The government awarded IBM the contract to maintain the employment records of 26 million people for Social Security.

In the meantime, although IBM had used the word *computing* in their original name, the machines we now know as computers were not developed until the 1940s. IBM's early contribution was to the huge computers of that time.

Forty years later, when personal computers came along, IBM made an historic deal. They manufactured their original personal computers (or PCs) in 1981, with DOS (Disk Operating System) bought from a small thirty-two-person company called Microsoft.

Thomas Watson, head of IBM, was quoted in 1943 as saying, "I think there is a world market for maybe five computers." Hmm, maybe he underestimated just a bit.

FAST FACT

A Good Harvest

What do Apple computers have to do with apples? Nothing. So why do they share a name with the fruit?

The two founders of the company, Steve Jobs and Steve Wozniak, took their famous brand name from the label of a record company whose music they liked.

They made their first Apple computers while working in Jobs's parents' garage in Los Altos, California, in 1976. The twenty-one-year-old Jobs and twenty-five-year-old Wozniak created the first personal computer that appealed to both businesses and the public. They were pioneers who realized that PCs were the wave of the future.

Speaking of the future, Apple later sponsored one of the most memorable television commercials in history. The ad introduced their Macintosh computers (whose name was taken from a real apple). The commercial that aired during the 1984 Super Bowl was so strange and futuristic many viewers wondered what it was all about. (Hint: If you've ever read George Orwell, note the year for its inspiration.) But others got the message. Something new and powerful was on the market. More than 70,000

Macs were sold in the next 100 days, and sales would soon hit $2 billion.

That revolutionary commercial—still talked about in advertising circles—cost more than $1 million and was only broadcast once.

The Internet has spawned all sorts of abbreviations—and many people freely use them without a second thought as to what they represent. Let's demystify. URL is "uniform resource locator." CD-ROM is "compact disk-read only memory." FTP is "file transfer protocol." PDF is "portable document format." DSL is "digital subscriber line." HTML is "hypertext markup language." HTTP is "hypertext transfer protocol." E-mail is "electronic mail." IT is "information technology." And JPEG is "joint photographic experts group."

FAST FACT

Hooray!

Jerry Yang and David Filo, students at Stanford University in the early 1990s, became frustrated at how difficult it was to negotiate the exciting but complicated World Wide Web. Together they worked to build a program that would organize Web sites into categories.

When Jerry and David started the Web's first search engine, it had the rather plain name of Jerry's Guide. That name didn't last long.

The team decided to choose an anti-establishment moniker and came up with "Yet Another Hierarchical Officious Oracle!" If you take the first letter of each of those words you get *Yahoo!*

Yahoo! went online in 1994, marking a significant milestone of the computer age.

How Do You Say "One Followed by 100 Zeroes"?

In 1938, nine-year-old Milton Sirotta asked his uncle, who was a mathematician, what the number one followed by 100 zeroes was called. His uncle, Edward

Kaiser, explained that there was no such word. Young Sirotta came up with *googol*, and the word is now accepted in the mathematical world.

Fast forward to 1995. Twenty-three-year-old Sergey Brin and twenty-four-year-old Larry Page met while working toward their doctorates in computer science at Stanford University. They embarked on a research project to develop technology for a fast search engine. By 1998, they were ready to start a company, using Larry's dorm room as their data center and Sergey's as their business office. Aiming for millions of hits on their Web site, they named the company Google— a play on the word "googol."

After being encouraged by fellow Stanford students, Yahoo! founders Jerry Yang and David Filo, Brin and Page moved their operations to a friend's garage in Menlo Park, California. There they built Google into a Web super-giant—the site now receives more than 200 million search queries every day.

World's Largest Bookstore Set Up in a Garage

With a degree in computer science from Princeton University, Jeff Bezos developed computer systems for New York financial institutions in the early 1990s. But he became bored and searched for something more exciting.

He and his wife decided to leave the East Coast and start life anew. They drove their Chevy Blazer west, and it was during their cross-country trip that Bezos conceived the idea of selling books on the World Wide Web. He concluded that no single bookstore was large enough to stock all the titles in print.

Because the idea of an online superstore seemed to hold such vast possibilities, Bezos named his venture after the most massive river in the world, the Amazon.

When the couple reached Seattle, they rented a house and set up Amazon.com in their garage. (What is it about garages in the computer world? Google, Hewlett-Packard, Apple, and Amazon all began in West Coast home garages.)

Bezos sold his first book on the Web in 1995. Within two years, he was selling millions of dollars worth of books, and revolutionized the world of retailing in the process. By December, 1999, *Time* magazine named Bezos its Person of the Year, calling him the "king of cybercommerce."

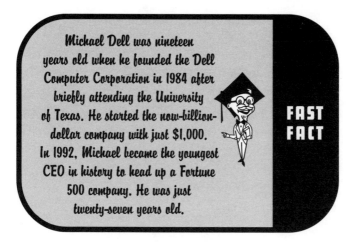

Michael Dell was nineteen years old when he founded the Dell Computer Corporation in 1984 after briefly attending the University of Texas. He started the now-billion-dollar company with just $1,000. In 1992, Michael became the youngest CEO in history to head up a Fortune 500 company. He was just twenty-seven years old.

FAST FACT

The Old Men

Long before today's computer world was a twinkle in someone's eye, Bill Hewlett and Dave Packard started the Hewlett-Packard Company.

It was 1939. Bill and Dave, classmates at Stanford University, founded their company in a rented garage in Palo Alto, California. There they made electronic equipment. Their first product was an audio oscillator. They sold eight to Walt Disney for the innovative sound system for the movie *Fantasia*.

Other electronic products followed, leading to the company's first computer in 1966 and its first personal computer in 1980.

By the time computers became commonplace in homes and offices, Bill and Dave were older men—much, much older than the likes of Michael Dell, Bill Gates, Steve Jobs, and Steve Wozniak, the emerging superstars of the computer age.

Dave died in 1996, and Bill in 2001. Their old rented garage has now been designated as an official California landmark.

Hobby Becomes $14 Billion Business

Pierre Omidyar is a computer guy through and through. He studied computer science at Tufts University in Medford, Massachusetts, and upon graduation in 1988, got a job with Apple computers.

On many evenings after returning from his day job, Pierre toyed with a computer hobby—setting up and running an auction site for person-to-person trading.

At first he called it, casually, eShop. But when he realized he was on to something big, he decided to establish the site as a full-time business.

Pierre relocated the business to the San Francisco Bay area in 1995, and renamed it eBay. The company grew rapidly. It now lists more than 16 million items for sale in 27,000 categories each day, and claims more than $14 billion in sales each year.

The Two-Word Campaign

According to advertising experts, one of the most effective campaigns of all time was also one of the shortest—just two words.

The magic words, "Intel inside," developed brand identity and demand for Intel, the company that invented the world's first microprocessor

Intel was founded in 1968 by Bob Noyce and Gordon Moore under the name of NM Electronics, the *N* and *M* standing for Noyce and Moore, respectively. In many ways the company paved the way for the computer revolution. Two years after the company was founded, the named was changed to the now-familiar Intel, taking *Int* from Integrated and *el* from electronics.

Intel has grown to be such a driving force that it captures more than 80 percent of today's consumer market, with $30 billion a year in revenues.

Andy Grove, who joined Noyce and Moore short-ly after the company was founded, went on to become CEO and was named *Time* magazine's Person of the Year in 1997, thereby certifying Intel's place in the computer revolution.

He Turned His Back on Billions of Dollars

Imagine inventing something that's used by millions of people every day, and then voluntarily choosing not to profit from it.

A young British computer scientist did just that. Tim Berners-Lee created the World Wide Web in 1990. He invented it while working for a physics lab in Geneva, Switzerland, where he developed a global system of linking documents across the Internet to help physicists share information stored on different computers.

Berners-Lee could have parlayed his invention into incredible wealth. But he decided to become an advocate for easy, inexpensive, unrestricted use of the Web—essentially giving it away. He said any attempt to make the Web proprietary would undermine its purpose.

After turning down lucrative commercial offers for the Web, he took a job as a computer researcher at Massachusetts Institute of Technology. Not only did he turn his back on all the money he could have made, but he never achieved worldwide fame. Many people who use the Web have never heard of Berners-Lee.

His was a rare case of a man setting a social and economic milestone for love, not money.

Much like Tim Berners-Lee, the inventor of the World Wide Web, Steve Dorner, the inventor who made e-mail possible, became neither rich nor famous. Dorner created the software for e-mail while working for the computing staff at the University of Illinois. The university gave the software away. Dorner was paid a salary but nothing more—no stock and no royalties.

FAST FACT

Eat and Run:
Fast Foods

Remember Melinda

*W*hen Melinda Thomas was growing up in Dublin, Ohio, in the 1960s, her family and friends never called her Melinda.

She was known by her nickname, Wendy—and you can probably guess what famous brand name she inspired.

When her dad, Dave Thomas, started his hamburger chain, he considered a lot of names for his fast food restaurants. In the end, he chose one close to his heart—his young daughter's nickname. The first Wendy's restaurant opened in Columbus, Ohio in 1969.

Wendy was eight years old when her name first went up in lights.

The Bell in Taco Bell

Glen Bell opened a hot dog stand in his hometown of San Bernardino, California, in 1948. In that same town, at that same time, two brothers named McDonald opened their first hamburger stand. From those humble beginnings in San Bernardino, both Bell and the McDonalds would see their names spread across the world in the fast food industry.

However, Bell didn't stay in the hot dog business. He had always been a fan of Mexican food and loved tacos, but realized there was no place to get quick taco service. So Bell worked out a fast-food system of pre-frying the shells and began selling 19¢ take-out tacos.

He called his stand Taco Tias. Then, as he opened more locations, he switched to El Tacos. But by 1962, Bell changed the name to include his own—and the brand known as Taco Bell was born.

A New Idea for Restaurants

California businessman Roy Allen bought a root beer formula from an Arizona pharmacist in 1919 and began selling mugs of the drink at a stand in Lodi, California. That led to a new fast-food concept.

Allen opened a second root beer stand in Sacramento, California, in 1920. He added some food and, capitalizing on the growing popularity of automobiles, made it a drive-in restaurant with what he called *tray boys* for curbside and takeout service.

It was reputed to be the world's first drive-in restaurant.

Meantime, Allen took in a partner, Frank Wright, and named his root beer after their last-name initials, creating the A&W root beer brand.

The A&W beverage and A&W restaurant chain grew in California, then throughout the West and Midwest, and after World War II, spread nationally and internationally.

In this day of many drive-in eateries, A&W has the claim of starting the trend and pioneering the fast-food drive-through service idea.

Walk the Plank . . . Straight to the Bank!

A peg-legged pirate in Robert Louis Stevenson's classic novel *Treasure Island* was the inspiration for

America's largest quick-service seafood chain. The restaurants are named Long John Silver's after Stevenson's infamous pirate.

The chain began with one restaurant in 1968, named Long John Silver's Fish 'n' Chips. The "Fish 'n' Chips" part of the name was dropped as the chain expanded and more varieties of food were offered, including chicken, sandwiches, salads, and desserts.

But most Long John Silver's are still designed with nautical and wharf-side themes in keeping with their original menus. The chain says it serves 45 million pounds of fish a year in its more than 1,200 units worldwide.

Stevenson, who lived from 1850 to 1894, wrote his *Treasure Island* adventure story in 1883 on a South Sea island in Western Samoa. Undoubtedly he never imagined that his villain would lend his name to a fast-food restaurant.

The Brothers Weren't Around When Their Name Went Worldwide

Who could have imagined what phenomenon would follow after brothers Maurice and Richard McDonald opened a simple hamburger stand in San Bernardino, California, in 1948?

Well, there was one man who could—Ray Kroc of Chicago.

Kroc was part owner of a milkshake-maker called the Multimixer. He heard that the McDonalds had bought eight Multimixers and wondered how such a small business would have need for so many shake-makers.

He paid a visit to Maurice and Richard's stand one day and was impressed with the way they were selling burgers and shakes in a fast-paced assembly line operation. Inspired, Kroc suggested they open other restaurants together—but the McDonald brothers weren't interested.

Undeterred, Kroc decided to buy out Maurice and Richard. He kept their last name, and beneath two golden arches sold billions of burgers across the country, and then around the world.

A Sandwich, and a Dream

Seventeen-year-old Fred DeLuca had just graduated from high school in 1965 in Bridgeport, Connecticut, and was trying to round up some money so he could go to college.

He called on a family friend, Dr. Peter Buck, hoping the doctor would give him a loan. Dr. Buck had a different idea. He told Fred he should open a shop that sold submarine sandwiches, and earn some money that way. The doctor offered him $1,000 to get started, and said he'd be his business partner.

Fred decided to take him up on his offer. He came up with the name *Subway* for his submarine sandwich shop.

The good idea became good business.

By 1974, Fred and Dr. Beck owned sixteen Subway shops in Connecticut. Fred went looking for money again. But this time, he sought investors as franchisees for his Subway stores.

That was another good idea. Today there are more than 17,000 Subway shops throughout seventy-one countries.

Perhaps the original opportunity was the only education Fred needed.

Curiously, Not from Kentucky

Kentucky Colonel Harland Sanders, the mastermind behind Kentucky Fried Chicken, wasn't a Kentuckian at all.

Sanders was born and raised in Henryville, Indiana.

As an adult, Sanders drifted from job to job, finally winding up as a restaurant cook in Corbin, Kentucky. There he developed his original recipe for Kentucky Fried chicken, using a top-secret blend of eleven herbs and spices.

In 1955, at age sixty-five, Sanders hit the road and began offering restaurants his prized chicken recipe for a small percentage of sales.

That was the beginning of franchising his Kentucky Fried Chicken. It proved successful and a group of investors bought Sanders out—but kept him as the spokesman and image for the company. Governor Ruby Laffoon even made him an official Kentucky colonel "in recognition for his contribution to the state's cuisine."

Today the company, now known as KFC, has more than 11,000 restaurants in eighty countries. Sanders himself died in 1980 at age ninety, but you still see this ex-Hoosier in KFC's logo and ads.

No Price
for Comfort

David Edgerton and James McLamore started the first Burger King restaurant in Miami, Florida, in 1954.

At the time Burger King's hamburgers cost 18¢—a not-so-unusual price in those days. In fact, when McDonald's started in the 1940s, they originally sold their hamburgers for 15¢ each. (During the Depression of the 1930s, the original national hamburger chain, White Tower, priced their burgers at, if you can believe it, 5¢ each! But we digress…)

Burger King brought a different major innovation to its industry. At early fast food restaurants, customers had three dining options—eat standing up, perch on stools, or take their food to go. Today it may seem like the most obvious of developments, but Burger King was responsible for creating the first fast food dining rooms. They gave customers a place to sit on chairs, relax, and enjoy their all-beef patties. So we can thank Burger King for all the wiped-down booths and bright Formica tables we commonly associate with fast food establishments.

Dominic & Nick
Open a Pizza Shop

Two guys named Dominic and Nick owned a neighborhood pizza shop in Ypsilanti, Michigan, in 1960 called DomiNick's.

With a $500 loan, Tom Monaghan and his brother Jim bought control of the shop. Jim stayed for a while, but then decided to trade his half ownership for the title to Tom's Volkswagen Beetle. (Hey, it seemed like a good idea at the time.)

Tom changed the store's name slightly, from DomiNick's to Domino's, and began building a major pizza chain. But that name change wasn't easy. As Tom started opening other Domino's pizza places around Michigan, the well-established Domino Sugar Company sued for trademark infringement.

After several court battles, the sugar company lost—and Domino's Pizza was allowed to keep its name. It now has more than 7,000 outlets, including some 2,000 outside the U.S., and sells more than $3 billion worth of pizza a year.

That's pretty sweet (though not sugary) success!

Clever College Boys

It seems hard to believe now, but before World War II, most Americans never ate pizza. What little pizza was sold and consumed in the U.S. was largely confined to Italian neighborhoods in big cities. In the rest of country, there were no pizza shops, and no pizza delivery.

That all began to change after the war, when GIs, returning from fighting in Italy, brought home an appetite for pizza. Pizza's popularity slowly began to grow in the 1950s—and two college boys saw a golden opportunity.

Frank and Don Carney were young brothers who dreamed of opening a pizza shop. They just *knew* pizza was a wave of the future. But they didn't have the start-up money. Lucky for them, their mother came to the rescue and loaned them $600.

Their first pizza parlor opened in Wichita, Kansas in 1958. And the name they chose for it? Pizza Hut.

Lots of Bucks for This Brand

Starbucks wasn't always on every street corner. In fact, the coffee company founded by Jerry Baldwin, Gordon Bowker, and Zev Siegl was just a small Seattle business providing coffee to local restaurants with only one store of its own, in Seattle's Pike Place Market.

But then in 1982 the company made a crucial move. It hired a man named Howard Schultz as director of retail operations.

Schultz took a fateful trip to Italy and was immediately impressed with the espresso bars he saw in Milan. There he watched Italians socializing over the caffeine and wanted to take the idea home. America, he felt, was ready for coffee bar culture.

On Schultz's return to the U.S., his enthusiasm convinced the Starbucks founders to test the coffee bar concept. Schultz opened the first one in Seattle in 1985 under the Starbucks name.

The city's citizens took to it and it became a huge success. Starbucks expanded with shops in Chicago and Vancouver, Canada—and then to more and more locations. With more than 7,000 Starbucks coffee bars around the world, the Italian example became a fixture of American culture.

Real or Fictitious?

She Doesn't Look
a Day Over 100

Aunt Jemima was real—but not really real.

Ms. Jemima dates back to 1889 in St. Joseph, Missouri, where Chris Rutt, a local newspaperman, experimented with packaging pancake mixes.

Rutt loved pancakes and was looking for a name for his product when a minstrel show came to St. Joseph. The show featured two musicians in black-face who performed a song called "Aunt Jemima," a hit of the day. Rutt was so taken with the per-formance that he used the song name for his new pancake mix.

Rutt sold his business to the Davis Milling com-pany, and they staged a big promotion of the product at the Chicago World's Fair in 1893. The company hired Nancy Green, an African-American woman from Kentucky, to personify Aunt Jemima at the fair. There

Green cooked up thousands of pancakes for fairgoers, and was such a hit that she continued as the living "Aunt Jemima" for the next thirty years.

Perfect Penmanship

General Mills gets lots of letters from customers requesting recipes or asking for advice on cooking and food preparation. Betty Crocker answers those letters personally.

Betty began her work in the 1920s, but if you look at her picture today, you'll see she hasn't aged one bit. The reason is logical: There never was a person named Betty Crocker at General Mills.

The company created Betty more than eighty years ago to be its fictitious spokeswoman. The last name Crocker was chosen to honor a retiring company executive, William Crocker. The name Betty was selected because it sounded, as the company explained, "warm and friendly."

When General Mills began advertising on the radio, an actress provided Betty's voice, and an artist created her picture for use on packages, recipes, and in ads. Over the years Betty's picture has been altered to keep up with the times, and she seems to get younger and younger.

Betty's beautiful, distinctive signature? It was penned by a secretary in the corporate offices in 1921. It is still in use today.

Did Duncan Hines Concoct Those Cake Mixes?

No, but Duncan Hines was real, all right. Hines was a traveling salesman turned food critic. He was on the road so much, he began rating restaurants in the 1930s and writing books on his ratings.

When he gave a restaurant a good rating, he would present them a sign that said, "Recommended by Duncan Hines." An astute businessman, Hines realized the sign would make his name well known and increase the sales of his books.

Then in 1950, food manufacturer Roy Park made a deal with Hines. Park purchased Hines's name as a brand, and Duncan Hines Ice Cream was soon on the market, followed by other products. Six years later Procter & Gamble bought the brand for various P&G foods.

The line was eventually pared down to focus on cake mixes, and Aurora Foods acquired the brand in 1997.

Aurora's logo is a combination of the original "Recommended by Duncan Hines" restaurant sign along with a picture of a Hines book.

Hines himself died in 1959 but his name lives on.

FAST FACT

Three musical instruments are named after actual people.

The saxophone was named for a Belgian instrument maker, Adolphe Sax, who invented the saxophone in 1840.

The sousaphone was named after nineteenth-and-twentieth century American bandmaster and leader of the U.S. Marine band, John Philip Sousa.

And the spinet piano got its name from the sixteenth century Italian composer, Giovanni Spinetti.

Fruits Named After Them

Granny Smith apples were first cultivated in Australia by Maria Ann (Granny) Smith of New South Wales.

Bartlett pears are named for Enoch Bartlett, a Roxbury, Massachusetts, farmer.

Greengage plums got their name from Sir William Gage, an English botanist.

Temple oranges honor William Temple, the man who developed that variety.

Macintosh apples came to us from a Scottish immigrant who discovered those kinds of apples growing wild on his newly-settled Canadian farm. Mr. Macintosh's first name has been lost to history, but his apples haven't been.

Ms. Mentzer Makes a Name for Herself

Estée Mentzer was born in the Queens section of New York City in 1910. Twenty years later she married Joseph Lauder and became Estée Lauder.

That's not all she became. Estée reportedly would wind up as the richest self-made woman in the world.

She began her own company in 1946 with jars of skin cream developed by her uncle, who was a chemist. The big breakthrough came in 1953, with her introduction of Youth-Dew Beauty Oil. That same year she incorporated Estée Lauder, Inc.

Lauder built the company with such marketing plans as the liberal use of free samples to enhance name-recognition and demand, and through sales at top department stores.

The line of Estée Lauder products grew to include various fragrances and makeup and skin care products, grossing over $1 billion a year in sales.

As to Joseph Lauder, who gave Estée her last name, he became her business partner.

Call for Philip Morris

The giant Philip Morris company was helped in its growth by a little man.

Originated in England in the mid 1800s, the company was founded by a London tobacco dealer, Philip Morris.

He exported his cigarettes and cigars around the British Empire and to America. By 1919, U.S.

stockholders bought the company. It became a major cigarette manufacturer, and later a huge conglomerate including food and beer products.

One of its brands in the years before World War II was Philip Morris cigarettes, which used a small man in a giant ad campaign.

Two members of the company's ad agency, Milton Biow and Ken Goode, were sitting in the lobby of the New Yorker Hotel in 1933, when they heard a bellboy paging people, as was customary then. They got the idea to ask the bellhop to page a Mr. Philip Morris. The bellboy, a midget named Johnny Roventini, yelled out in his distinctive voice, "Call for Philip Mar-iss. Call for Philip Mar-iss."

The ad men knew they had something. They hired Roventini on the spot and used him in radio commercials. His picture, in his bellboy uniform, was splashed across magazine and newspaper ads. Little Johnny helped make Philip Morris big.

Hot Dog Dreams

Oscar Mayer—the man, not the wiener—was born in Bavaria in 1859, and came to the United States in

1873, after the failure of his family's meat business.

Oscar settled in Detroit, where he got a job as a butcher, then moved to Chicago to work for the Armour Meat Packing company.

Still in his twenties, he and two brothers, Gottfried and Max, opened their own small butcher shop on Sedgwick Street in the Windy City, naming it Oscar Mayer & Brothers.

They specialized in sausages and soon were manufacturing them at plants in both Chicago and Milwaukee.

Their business grew and in 1929, they became the first company to identify their sausages with a brand name, calling them, naturally, Oscar Mayer Wieners.

The brothers and Oscar's nephew, Carl, decided to wrap their wieners in a still well known yellow paper covering. And it was Carl who came up with the idea of the "Wienermobile" to promote the brand.

The popular jingle, "I'd love to be an Oscar Mayer Wiener" followed. Oscar was active in the business until he was ninety-six years old. He continued marketing his beloved sausages until a few days before his death in 1955.

Eight-Year-Old Girl
Becomes Brand Name

In 1935, thirty-two-year-old Charlie Lubin bought a small neighborhood bakery store in Chicago, and over the next twelve years expanded it into a chain of seven shops.

By 1949, his bakeries had developed a special cheesecake that proved to be very popular.

Charlie branded the cheesecake with the name of his eight-year-old daughter. He called it Sara Lee Cheesecake.

Other sweet products followed, including pound cakes and coffeecakes. Their popularity and the advent of frozen foods gave Charlie the idea to ship his products to other cities.

Lubin eventually expanded his shipments to forty-eight states—and changed the brand to "From the Kitchens of Sara Lee."

In 1968, Mitch Lee, writer of the Broadway hit "Man of La Mancha," composed the jingle "Nobody does it like Sara Lee," that became a long-lasting, popular ad campaign and slogan. (It was only a coincidence that Mitch Lee's last name is the same as Sara Lee's middle name.)

And what became of the real Sara Lee? As of 2004, she's a sixty-three-year-old grandmother who, the company says, loves to spend time on her computer—probably while nibbling on some Sara Lee goodies.

A Lifetime of Popcorn

From early childhood until old-age death, one man's life revolved around popcorn. Naturally, his name became a popcorn brand.

The story begins on an Indiana farm in 1907, where Orville Redenbacher was born. His father grew, what else, corn. As soon as he was old enough, young Orville made spending money by popping and selling popcorn in the area.

As a teenager, Orville worked with his father to develop hybrid corn that would pop lighter, fluffier, and tastier.

At age seventeen he won a local competition for experiments with corn.

When he got to Purdue University, it's no surprise that he studied techniques in corn growing and popping in the agricultural school.

As an adult, he formed the Orville Redenbacher Gourmet Popcorn Company.

Hunt-Wesson bought the company in 1976, but Orville stayed on as a spokesman, with his name and face used on packages and in ads. Orville died at age eighty-eight in 1995, knowing that his beloved popcorn was a top brand.

The Name Game

Dr. Joseph Lawrence of St. Louis created a new product in 1880—an antibacterial liquid to be used as a mouthwash and gargle.

He could have named his product after himself, but instead, he chose to honor another physician.

There was a doctor in England who had become well known for pioneering ideas in fighting germs and infections and in developing the emerging science of bacteriology.

This celebrated germ fighter was Joseph Lister. Dr. Lawrence decided to name his new antibacterial product Listerine (the *ine* was a common suffix for medical products then).

The question is, did Lawrence forgo using his own name on the product to honor a worthy colleague, or did he think he'd have better sales using the more famous Lister's name? We'll never know, but regardless, Listerine became a major brand.

A Long Shot

A young mother enjoyed making cookies and people really seemed to like them, so she decided to open a cookie store in Palo Alto, California, in 1977.

Her friends tried to talk her out of it. She had no business experience, they said, and they told her she couldn't make any money just selling cookies.

But she went ahead anyway.

The name of this young mother: Debbi Fields. Debbi decided to call her store by her last name, and it became Mrs. Fields Chocolate Chippery.

She quickly proved her friends wrong.

So good was business in the early days, Debbi began franchising her name and cookies. Today there are Mrs. Fields stores in virtually every U.S. state with more than 600 locations. A line of baked goods was added to the cookies.

In 1992, Mrs. Fields went international. Her franchises can be found in eleven foreign countries.

He Performs Feats with Feet

William Scholl had a thing about feet, and turned his name into a multimillion-dollar brand.

Scholl's grandfather was a shoemaker. Young William began his fascination with feet by using his grandpa's tools to repair shoes.

During his first job, in a Chicago shoe store in 1900, he saw that people had all kinds of trouble with their feet, and not much available to help them. Sensing he'd found his calling, William enrolled in night classes at a local medical school, focusing his studies on the foot.

By day, William began making products such as arch supporters, cushioned insoles, and corn pads. When he got his medical degree, he had the brand name he wanted—Dr. Scholl.

A tenacious businessman, Scholl developed creative ways to sell his foot-care items. He offered commissions to shoe salesmen who pushed his products. He ran a Cinderella Foot Contest and sponsored a national walking race.

The investment paid off. He became a millionaire in 1915 at age thirty-three.

By the time he died in 1968, the real Dr. Scholl had built the Dr. Scholl brand into a nearly $100 million company.

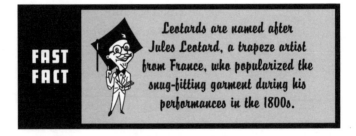

FAST FACT

Leotards are named after Jules Leotard, a trapeze artist from France, who popularized the snug-fitting garment during his performances in the 1800s.

Candy of Many Colors

Necco candy wafers were not named for any particular person. They got their name from the company that makes them—the New England Confectionery Company. The *Nec* of *Necco* comes from the first letters of New England Confectionery, and the *co* from the abbreviation of the word *company*. Neccos have been made for more than 100 years in the Boston area.

Who Was Dow Jones?

There was a newspaper reporter in New York who specialized in business news. In 1882 he decided to go out on his own, and rented a small basement office. There he wrote about the latest happenings on Wall Street and delivered his reports on mimeographed sheets to brokers around the city each day.

That was the beginning of the *Wall Street Journal.*

This enterprising reporter also established the first statistical measure of stocks, which became known as the Dow Jones average.

The man's name, however, wasn't Dow Jones. It was Charles Dow. But he had two partners: One was Edward Jones, and the other was Charles Bergstresser.

When they formed their company they decided to use Dow and Jones's last names, but not Bergstresser's. It's not known why they left Bergstresser out, but by doing so, they saved everybody from struggling with a mouthful!

FAST FACT

The collarless sweaters that button down the front were named for a man who popularized them, England's Earl of Cardigan. Besides having a sweater style named for him, Cardigan is remembered for leading the famous Charge of the Light Brigade in 1854 during the Crimean War.

Alas, Cardigan survived bloody battles in foreign wars but died from injuries back home when he fell off his horse.

That Jean Sure Makes Nice Pants!

It would make a good story if someone named Jean started the custom of wearing blue jeans. But such is not the case.

The name instead came from a city. French weavers were employed to make denim work clothes in the Italian city of Genoa. The weavers called Genoa

Genes in French, and referred to their product by the same name. When the work clothes made their way into English-speaking areas, the term evolved into *jeans*.

Blue jeans were popularized in America by a seventeen-year-old immigrant tailor, Levi Strauss. Strauss arrived in San Francisco during the gold rush of the 1850s. He realized that miners needed work clothes, so began making denim pants for them—and made a discovery. He realized that if he dyed the neutral-colored denim blue, the dark color would minimize the appearance of dirt and stains.

Strauss's blue jeans became a hit with the miners, and eventually cowboys as well. It was the beginning of a very successful company: Levi's.

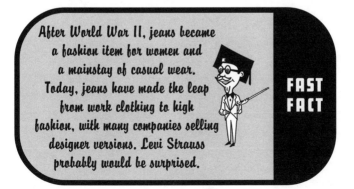

After World War II, jeans became a fashion item for women and a mainstay of casual wear. Today, jeans have made the leap from work clothing to high fashion, with many companies selling designer versions. Levi Strauss probably would be surprised.

FAST FACT

On the Road and In the Air

The Popular American Car
with a Foreign Name

Swiss-born Louis Chevrolet was a top driver in the early days of auto racing—a Jeff Gordon of his time.

William Durant, the founder of the General Motors Company, asked for Louis Chevrolet's help designing a car. His contribution didn't end there. Durant decided to use Chevrolet's name for the car because he felt it had a nice musical sound to it.

When the first Chevrolets were produced in 1911, people unfamiliar with the foreign pronunciation called them Chev-ro-LETs instead of Chev-ro-LAYs. Future advertising and popularity would correct that.

Unfortunately neither Durant nor Louis Chevrolet personally prospered from their creation. Durant lost control of General Motors and wound up bankrupt. Chevrolet sold his interest in the car and formed an aircraft company that failed.

In the 1930s, Louis Chevrolet was living in poverty. General Motors—apparently feeling guilty that the namesake of their most popular car was suffering financially—found room for him on the payroll.

As legend has it, after Chevrolet died in 1941, friends asked his widow what kind of car she was driving. She replied, "A Dodge."

Father-Daughter Bonding

When businessman Emil Jellinek began racing cars in Europe, he didn't want to use his own name. Instead, he raced under the name of his young daughter, calling himself, simply, Mercedes.

The racing career was successful, as were the cars, ordered specially from a man named Karl Benz. The two decided to form a manufacturing partnership. There was no question what they'd call their new cars: Mercedes-Benz. The name was trademarked in 1902, when Emil's daughter, Mercedes, was twelve years old.

But wait. Emil did more than that. He liked the name Mercedes so much, he changed his own name legally to Emil Jellinek-Mercedes, saying it was probably the first time a father had taken his daughter's name.

WHY THE "B," "M," AND "W" IN BMW?
Technically, the automobile brand's official name is Bayerische Motoren Werke.

The German translates to Bavarian Motor Works in English.

The company began in Bavaria, a state in southeastern Germany.

FAST FACT

How Datsun Became Nissan

In an unusual move, a major automaker changed its brand name—from Datsun to Nissan.

The company was formed in Japan in 1914 by three men whose family names began with *D, A,* and *T.* They took those three letters, added the Japanese suffix of *sun,* and called their first cars *Datsun.*

In 1931, Datsun was acquired by a company whose name was Nihon Sagyo, and whose stock exchange symbol was Ni-San.

The new company continued to make Datsuns,

but also added models they called *Nissans*, after their Ni-San symbol.

By 1980, after they entered the international market and scored a big success in America, they decided their cars should be known by just one name. They chose Nissan and slowly dropped Datsun.

From Cloth to Cars

A Japanese family named Toyoda started a textile mill in 1918, led by Eiji, Kiichiro, and Sakichi Toyoda.

Sakichi was the enterprising mechanical engineer of the bunch, and by 1929 he had designed special equipment to produce automobiles. In the 1930s, Toyoda officially left textiles and turned out cars for the Japanese market.

Although the Toyoda plant was bombed during World War II, the later occupying U.S. command urged the Toyodas to rebuild and make buses, trucks, and cars for Japan's post-war reconstruction.

The Toyodas did rebuild and soon created innovative production techniques that would be copied around the world. Toyoda cars were introduced to America in 1957 and the energy-efficient autos quickly captured a large share of the U.S. market, especially during the gasoline price hikes of the 1970s.

So why did the company change its name from Toyoda to Toyota? It was a marketing move, operating under the assumption that Toyota would sound better in English-language conversations and commercials. Well, something seems to have worked!

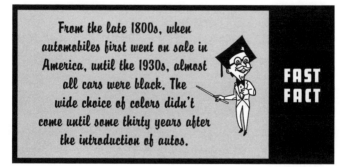

From the late 1800s, when automobiles first went on sale in America, until the 1930s, almost all cars were black. The wide choice of colors didn't come until some thirty years after the introduction of autos.

FAST FACT

The Cars Named After a God

Jujiro Matsuda started a tiny manufacturing company in Hiroshima, Japan in 1920, making cork products and then machine tools. By 1931 he was turning out small, three-wheeled trucks.

He became a full-fledged auto manufacturer in 1960, making a two-door coupe, and two years later, a four-door car.

In 1970, he began exporting his cars to the U. S., where they became a major brand. Matsuda named his automobiles after the highest god in the Zoroastrian religion—the god Ahura Mazda. Ahura Mazda is known as the Zoroastrianism god of reason, who grants wisdom and requires good deeds for help in the struggle against evil.

Mazda is the third car named for a god. Years earlier, the Ford Motor Company brought out the Mercury, named for the Roman god of travel; and later, General Motors introduced the Saturn, which shares its name with the Roman god of agriculture.

The Sad Story of David Buick

How would you like to have a car named after you?

It didn't do much good for David Buick.

Buick was a plumber who came to America from Scotland in the late 1800s. He was a good plumber, and invented a way to bond porcelain to iron—a process still used for bathtubs and sinks.

With the money he got for his invention, Buick switched to tinkering with automobiles in the early days of the industry. In 1903, he found backers and started a car company that he named after himself.

But while Buick cars are still around, David Buick didn't last long in the business. By 1906, the Buick Motor Car Company suffered financial problems, and David was forced out of his namesake enterprise.

Things went from bad to worse for David. What money he had left soon dried up after a series of bad investments in oil and land. In the end, David didn't have enough money to buy a car—even one with his name on it.

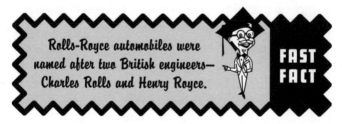

Rolls-Royce automobiles were named after two British engineers—Charles Rolls and Henry Royce.

FAST FACT

He Had His Hands in Everything

Walter Chrysler had a career like nobody else in automotive history. Name a U.S. car brand, and Chrysler likely put his mark on it.

As a young man from Kansas in the early 1900s, he became interested in the budding automobile business, and took a job as a manager with the Buick Company in 1912. Four years later, he was named president of Buick.

From there, he became a vice president at General Motors, working with Chevrolets, Pontiacs, Oldsmobiles, and Cadillacs. And then he moved on to the Willys-Overland Company and was made president of the famous Maxwell cars.

At that point Chrysler thought it was time he had a company of his own. In 1924, he founded and became president of the Chrysler Corporation—the company that went on to make Dodges, Plymouths, Imperials, Valiants, and, of course, Chryslers.

Chrysler stayed with his company until his death in 1940. In his lifetime, he worked with twelve other American brands—nearly all the big ones but Ford.

His success proved that thirteen could be a very lucky number.

The Dodge Boys

Brothers Horace and John Dodge started their careers making bicycles in Detroit, but then decided to move from two wheels to four. In 1914, they made one of the very first cars with an all-steel body.

Success proved quick, but alas, short-lived. Both Dodge brothers died six years after launching their brand of automobiles.

Dodge ceased to be an independent company when it was sold to Chrysler in 1928.

Although Nash cars are no longer made, they did establish a milestone in auto safety. Nash was the first automobile to include seat belts, in 1950.

FAST FACT

The Man Named Honda

When Soichiro Honda formed a company in Japan after World War II, it wasn't to manufacture his now well-known automobiles.

Honda exclusively made motorcycles for the Japanese market. Few then would have guessed that eventually he would turn out the best-selling car in America.

In fact, when Honda did enter the U.S. market in 1959, it was still only as a small motorcycle manufacturer. It wasn't until the 1960s that Honda began making automobiles—automobiles that so many in America wanted.

By 1990, American purchases of the Honda Accord exceeded those of any other car. And to this day the Accord and the Honda Civic regularly appear among the Top 5 of U.S. sales.

Due to his success, Soichiro Honda was the first Asian to be inducted in the U.S. Automotive Hall of Fame. Not bad for a onetime mechanic who did not originally intend to make cars.

FAST FACT

Some historians consider Ransom E. Olds to be the true founder of the automobile industry. He built the first auto factory, was the first to mass-produce cars, and sold the first American-made cars overseas.

He named his first product—the Oldsmobile—after himself, and produced REO cars (later, better known as trucks), using his initials for the brand name.

Pick a Color

Ever wonder why taxicabs are yellow?

Believe it or not, almost all cars and taxis were black in the 1920s. John Hertz owned a taxicab company in Chicago at that time and was looking for a way to make his cabs stand out from the competition. Hertz decided to paint his taxis a distinctive color.

He went to the University of Chicago and asked them to make a study of what color was the easiest to see at a distance.

The result was yellow, and thus the tradition of yellow taxis began.

In the meantime, ever-resourceful Hertz had another idea. There were cars sitting in his company garage that hadn't been converted to taxis yet. Why not offer his excess autos to people who wanted to rent a car for a brief time?

Adding to his fleet by buying out a man who had started a small rental operation, Hertz went on to create the first major car-rental company in the United States.

The Hertz Rent-A-Car company still uses yellow as its corporate color.

FAST FACT

Limousines got their name from the Limousin region of France, where they were first made.

Winged Transportation?

Hertz's major competitor—Avis—didn't enter the rent-a-car business until more than two decades after Hertz began.

After World War II there was a vast increase in air travel, and a man who saw the growing need for car rentals at airports started Avis in 1946.

Cars were first made available at the Detroit, Michigan, airport, soon thereafter at other airports, and finally at other non-airport locations around the country.

There's a popular misconception about how Avis' name was chosen. With the similarity of *Avis* to *aves*—the scientific classification of birds—you'd think it had something to do with flying, and such words as *aviary* and *aviation*. Since Avis was originally created for travelers at airports, many assumed that's how the company derived its name.

But the truth is simpler. The founder of the company who envisioned the future of air travel and car rentals gave his name to the company. He was William Avis.

Bye-Bye Brands

Since the start of the automobile age, some 2,000 companies have made nearly 5,000 brands of cars in America, but the vast majority are no longer produced.

Some famous names of cars that are long gone are the Stutz-Bearcat, Pierce-Arrow, Cord, Auburn, Austin, Chalmers, Crosley, Essex, Graham-Paige, Columbia, Franklin, Hupmobile, Lafayette, LaSalle, Marmon, Stanley Steamer, Peerless, Maxwell, and Dusenberg.

Dusenbergs were so popular in the 1920s that the expression "It's a doozie," became a cool way to describe anything pleasing.

In more recent times, production ceased on such once well-known brands as Packard, Desoto, Studebaker, Nash, Plymouth, and Oldsmobile.

Among the more colorful names of car brands in the early part of the twentieth century were the Buzmobile, the Zip, and (how can we forget?) the O-We-Go.

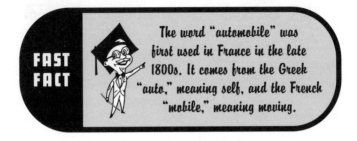

FAST FACT

The word "automobile" was first used in France in the late 1800s. It comes from the Greek "auto," meaning self, and the French "mobile," meaning moving.

Good Ol' Gray Truck

Carl Wickman owned an old, battered gray truck, and decided to make some money from it. He started hauling workers to and from their jobs at the ore mines of northern Minnesota in 1914.

Business was good, so he opted to buy more vehicles to transport not only workers but anyone needing to travel between small Minnesota towns.

Before long, Wickman had created a bus company. For its name, he chose to honor his original gray truck. The Greyhound bus company was born, and used greyhound dogs as its symbol.

One problem: There has always been confusion about the spelling of gray and grey. The preferred correct spelling for the color is *gray*, while the dogs name is correctly spelled *greyhound*.

That apparently didn't bother Wickman. Even

though his beloved truck was gray, he stuck with the good brand name of Greyhound for his buses.

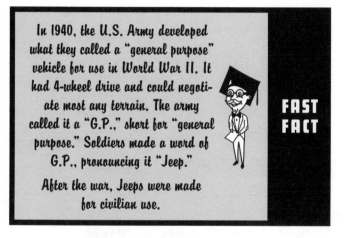

In 1940, the U.S. Army developed what they called a "general purpose" vehicle for use in World War II. It had 4-wheel drive and could negotiate most any terrain. The army called it a "G.P.," short for "general purpose." Soldiers made a word of G.P., pronouncing it "Jeep."

After the war, Jeeps were made for civilian use.

FAST FACT

One of These Things Is Not Like the Other . . .

Ever looked up at that giant yellow seashell looming over a Shell gas station and wondered what in the world shells have to do with gasoline? Actually, a lot.

What became the megalithic Shell Oil Company all started in a little novelty shop in London in the early 1800s. The proprietor, Marcus Samuel, collected seashells, painted them pretty colors, and sold them.

Business was good and Marcus's store became known as The Shell Shop. He discovered he could do more business by getting shells from other countries, so he started an import-export company. He'd import shells from around the world—and for exports, he began buying up kerosene and shipping it to the far reaches of the British Empire. With the kerosene trade added to his company, he changed its name from The Shell Shop to Shell Transport and Trading.

From this humble beginning, the Shell Oil Company evolved. They didn't forget their roots. A picture of a seashell is still used in their logo.

The Mystery of Diesel

Rudolf Diesel, born in Paris of German parents, became a mechanical engineer who would give the world the diesel engine and diesel fuel.

Diesel began working on his engine in the early 1890s, and came close to dying as a result. His first engine exploded, almost killing him, but it proved that fuel could be ignited without a spark.

Diesel went on to perfect his engine and patented it in 1897. He then founded a factory to make the engines he named after himself, and it looked like he was set for a successful life. But tragedy and mystery entered the scene.

On a German ship bound for England in 1913, Diesel disappeared and was never seen again. No evidence was ever found that Diesel might have died in an accident, suicide, or by foul play. His disappearance remains one of the world's unexplained mysteries.

> You might think that AC sparkplugs got their name from the abbreviation of alternating current. But that had nothing to do with it. AC sparkplugs were named from the initials of their inventor, Albert Champion.

FAST FACT

What Happened to the First American Auto Brand?

If anyone in America deserves to have a car named after him, it would be the person who built and sold the first successful automobiles.

Actually, that honor goes to two people, brothers Charles and Frank Duryea, who produced the first gasoline-powered cars in the United States.

The brothers began making cars in Springfield, Massachusetts, in 1891, and organized the Duryea Motor Wagon Company.

Their Duryea cars did well. A Duryea model won the first auto race ever held in America, a fifty-two-mile race on Thanksgiving Day in 1895, from Chicago to Waukegan, Illinois. The Duryea brothers collected the first prize of $2,000.

Duryea cars stayed in production unti1 1918, when the company went out of business. Unlike other auto pioneers such as Henry Ford, the Duryeas, sadly, have no car named after them today.

FAST FACT

The word "motel" entered the English language when Arthur Heinman combined the words "motor" and "hotel," and opened the world's first motel in San Luis Obispo, California, in 1925.

Barely Passing

When Fred Smith was a student at Yale in 1966, he came up with what some said was a crazy idea.

The idea was a revolutionary delivery system. Letters and packages would be picked up across the country and loaded into planes. The planes would then fly to one central location, arriving around 11:00 P.M. The letters and packages would be unloaded from the planes and sorted—and then put back on planes by 4:00 A.M. for delivery the next day.

Smith used that idea as the basis of his economics class term paper. His professor was unimpressed and gave him a C.

After service in Vietnam, Smith raised money and plunged ahead with his idea, although people again told him he was crazy. Determined to prove it could be done, Smith selected Memphis, Tennessee, for his landing and loading site. He picked Memphis because it's more-or-less centrally located in the U.S. (based on population), and the weather there is rarely bad enough to close the airport.

At age twenty-nine in 1973, Smith launched his new company. He called it Federal Express (now FedEx). With his overnight delivery service, Smith originated a new industry—despite the C on his term paper.

FAST FACT

FedEx operates a force of more than 600 aircraft. Some countries don't have as many planes in their air force.

The World's First Stewardesses

The brand known as United Airlines came by its name honestly. It was formed by uniting several small airlines of the 1920s into one company—but United's biggest claim to fame was their introduction of female flight attendants.

Before United put women employees in the air in 1930, the few flight attendants then used by some airlines were all men (they were often called *cabin boys*). Their main job was to handle baggage and check tickets on board (there was no passing through security before boarding then).

Enter Ellen Church, a registered nurse, who suggested that United use nurses to look after passengers during flights. United bought the idea and hired eight nurses to work as what they called *stewardesses*. Ms. Church was given the honor of becoming the world's first stewardess when she was chosen to fly from Oakland, California, to Chicago, Illinois, on May 15, 1930.

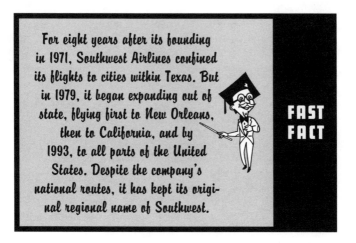

For eight years after its founding in 1971, Southwest Airlines confined its flights to cities within Texas. But in 1979, it began expanding out of state, flying first to New Orleans, then to California, and by 1993, to all parts of the United States. Despite the company's national routes, it has kept its original regional name of Southwest.

FAST FACT

Acrimony in the Air

When United Airlines and Ellen Church introduced stewardesses to air travel, there were some challenges. Some pilots complained about having to look after female crew members. And some pilots' wives began a letter writing campaign requesting the removal of the stewardesses.

The original work rules were tough. Stewardesses were told they had to give a "rigid military salute" when the pilot and co-pilot entered and left the plane, and they were also responsible for the pilots' personal luggage.

As for their own lives, stewardesses were not allowed to be married. The no-marriage rule at United lasted until November, 1968.

Eventually, the chilly reception given the first stewardesses warmed, and the women became an accepted —and expected—part of the airline industry. The word *stewardess* lasted into the 1960s and 1970s, when two factors ended its use. To avoid discrimination suits, airlines began hiring men to join women in the job; and a number of feminists declared the term *stewardess* sexist. Stewardesses evolved into what we now call *flight attendants.*

FAST FACT

As other airlines joined United in hiring stewardesses, they, too, employed nurses for the job. The theory was that nurses could better handle passengers' needs on the bumpy flights of the 1930s. As air travel became safer and smoother after the 1930s, a nursing background was no longer required.

They Served a Delta—
Then Became Delta Air Lines

The Huff Daland crop-dusting planes began operations in 1924 and together would grow to become a major, international airline.

Huff Daland planes were originally used to dust crops in the Mississippi Delta region, and later began carrying passengers and U.S. mail from Jackson, Mississippi, to Dallas, Texas, with stops in Shreveport and Monroe, Louisiana.

In 1928, C . E. Woolman took over Huff Daland and changed its name to Delta in recognition of the Delta region it served. Originally called Delta Air Service, it became Delta Air Lines in 1934.

The company eventually moved its headquarters from the Delta area to Atlanta, Georgia, in 1941, and began expanding its routes throughout the South and Southwest. It was in Atlanta that Delta pioneered the "hub and spoke system," with planes bringing passengers to the hub airport where they connected to other Delta flights.

Eventually, the former crop-dusting air service was flying travelers to New York, California, the Caribbean, London, and around the world.

Lindbergh's Legacy

On the morning of April 15, 1926, a young pilot by the name of Charles Lindbergh stowed a bag of U.S. mail on a little DH-4 biplane and took off from Chicago, Illinois to St. Louis, Missouri.

That was the initial flight of Robertson Airways, which had a government contract to carry the mail around the Midwest. Lindbergh was designated the chief pilot for Robertson, which employed two other pilots for their three-plane fleet.

Soon, both Robertson and Lindbergh would become better known.

Lindbergh, of course, just a year later, achieved international fame as the first person to fly solo across the Atlantic. In the Roaring Twenties there was perhaps no bigger international celebrity than Lindbergh.

In the meantime, Robertson merged with several other small airlines to form a company called American Airways, later known as American Airlines. By the end of the 1930s, American was the number one domestic air carrier in terms of passenger miles.

Major Name Changes

All-American Aviation began air service to small Pennsylvania and Ohio towns in 1939.

By 1953, the company changed its name to Allegheny Airlines in recognition of the Allegheny mountains and river that sat in the heart of its flight network.

But then Allegheny started expanding, gobbling up other airlines with names like Mohawk, Lake Central, Piedmont, and Pacific Southwest.

As they began flying coast-to-coast, the name *Allegheny* was no longer appropriate. In 1979, Allegheny Airlines became USAir.

That name seemed perfectly good, but by 1996, new management felt the company name should be changed again. Planes were repainted, a new logo was designed, signs at ticket counters were altered, new stationery was ordered, and publicity was rolled out—all for the slight change from USAir to US Airways.

The Man Who Changed Air Travel

Juan Trippe, CEO of Pan American Airlines, coined a phrase in 1951 that would alter air travel forever.

The phrase Trippe came up with was *tourist class*. Until then there had been just one class of air travel: first. And there had been just one fare level—as high as the market would bear.

Trippe realized that great masses of people had not yet become airplane travelers, in part because of the cost, in part because of the elitist first class image, and in part because of fear. Trippe's plan was to get—as someone said—the "peasants" to fly. To start, he offered tourist class on Pan Am's transatlantic flights, and then on domestic ones. Soon, the idea of bargain-priced travel spread throughout the industry.

When other airlines copied Trippe's tourist class idea, some used different names like economy class or coach class, but whatever it was called, it made air travel popular.

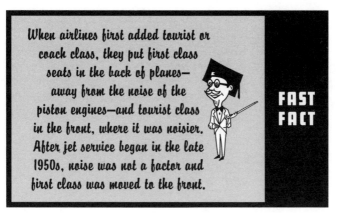

When airlines first added tourist or coach class, they put first class seats in the back of planes—away from the noise of the piston engines—and tourist class in the front, where it was noisier. After jet service began in the late 1950s, noise was not a factor and first class was moved to the front.

FAST FACT

Bill and Bertha

Bill Boeing made a fortune in real estate, buying and selling forestlands in Washington state in the early 1900s. The wealth gave him the opportunity to pursue his interest in a new thing called aviation.

Boeing had become fascinated with airplanes—and he began investigating how he could become part of the industry.

In 1916, Boeing started building some of the first planes designed for passengers. And while Bill built them, his wife, Bertha, happily christened them. During the 1920s, Bertha christened Bill's new planes with bottles of orange soda instead of champagne because of the Prohibition laws then in effect.

The Boeing Company grew to become one of the largest manufacturers of airplanes in the world. Other honors followed. In 1957, Boeing received an order for a 707 jet that would be called Air Force One when the U.S. President was aboard.

Trouble with Pronunciation

Allan and Malcolm Loughead got hooked on aviation when they first flew in a plane over San Francisco Bay in 1913.

Eventually they became builders of many of the world's best-known airplanes—but people had trouble pronouncing their name, so when they founded their company, they changed the name from Loug-head to the now-familiar Lockheed.

With pronunciation problems alleviated, Lockheed built the first plane to fly across the United States non-stop, the Lockheed Vega, in 1928.

In a Lockheed Vega, Amelia Earhart made history as the first woman to fly solo across the Atlantic in 1932. Another milestone was achieved in a Vega by Wiley Post, who made the first solo flight around the world in 1933.

By 1995, Lockheed merged with the Martin aircraft company to form the Lockheed Martin brand name. Martin had been founded by another aviation pioneer, Glenn Martin, who began building planes in 1909.

Northwest Airlines began as a mail carrier from Minneapolis to Chicago in 1926. Northwest is the name they chose despite the fact that the airline flew not in the Northwest, but in the Midwest.

FAST FACT

FAST FACT

Continental Airlines was named by owner Robert Six in 1936, despite the fact that it did not fly coast to coast at the time. Eventually Continental would grow from largely serving just western states to truly spanning the continent.

It's Easier to Say KLM

The initials in the Dutch airline KLM stand for Koninklijke-Luchtvaart-Maatschappij, which means Royal Airline Company.

Did you know that of all the airlines still operating in the world today, KLM is the oldest? It was founded in 1919. Its official name is the Royal Dutch airline, having been given that designation by Queen Wilhelmina of the Netherlands.

KLM has a unique name for its frequent flyer program. They call it the Flying Dutchman.

The First U.S. Air Service

The first regularly scheduled airplane passenger service in the United States was between not New York or Washington or Los Angeles or Chicago, but Tampa and St. Petersburg, Florida.

America's first commercial airline, making regular passenger flights, was started by Tony Jannus in 1914. He ran daily flights twenty-five miles across Tampa Bay, linking the cities of Tampa and St. Petersburg. The flights marked the beginning of the U.S. airline industry.

The first airline to offer jet service on domestic flights was National Airlines. The year was 1958. Before that all commercial airlines flew propeller planes on domestic routes. National's inaugural jet service was between New York and Miami.

FAST FACT

Odds and Ends

Teen Dreams

Jerry Siegel and Joe Shuster, classmates at Cleveland's Glenville High in 1934, conceived of the idea of Superman, but they had lives that proved to be anything but super.

In March 1938, in exchange for $130, they signed away all rights to Superman to DC Comics. When Superman proved an immediate sensation, Siegel and Shuster sought a share of the profits. They were rebuffed and lived the rest of their lives near poverty.

The Superman brand has earned more than $1 billion in movies, books, TV, and commercial products. Meanwhile, Siegel and Shuster had trouble making a living.

Late in life they finally did receive a $20,000 annuity from DC. Shuster, then blind, died in 1992.

Siegel, in an interview before his death in 1996, said, "I can't stand to look at Superman. It makes me physically ill."

Not a super life for creating a super brand.

Mega Mouse

When Walt Disney started his art career, he had no money for a nice studio. Undaunted, he found an old mice-infested garage in which to work. From that studio, he and one of the mice he used for inspiration would go on to fame and fortune.

But it's surprising to learn that Disney had a different name in mind for his mouse.

Disney was going to call his creation Mortimer Mouse. However, just before the mouse's first public appearance, Disney's wife, Lillian, convinced Walt not to use the name Mortimer.

Lillian thought that Mortimer sounded too formal, and it was she who suggested the mouse be called Mickey.

Mickey Mouse made his debut in an animated movie cartoon called *Steamboat Willie* in 1928. He went on to become a brand and industry unto himself.

DO AS I SAY, NOT AS I DO

For many years, male employees at Disney theme parks were forbidden to wear facial hair, including mustaches. It was an odd rule since Walt Disney himself always wore a mustache. The no-mustache rule for employees was finally rescinded in 2000.

FAST FACT

He Forgot His Money— and Look What We Got

A New York City lawyer, Frank McNamara, went out to dinner one night in 1950. At the conclusion of the meal, the waiter brought him a check, and McNamara was embarrassed to discover he had forgotten to bring any cash with him.

There were no credit cards for dining and most other purchases at that time. Before 1950, the only credit cards available were issued by a few gasoline companies and department stores, and were intended for use at their locations only.

The embarrassing episode prompted McNamara to invent the world's first general-use credit card. He called it the Diners Club card. It was originally honored at only a few New York restaurants, but the idea spread. Soon, more eating establishments signed up for it, and eventually many stores began to accept it.

The forgetful McNamara had created a whole new way of life for restaurants, retail stores, other businesses, and consumers all over the world. No longer would people have to take a lot of cash with them when they decided to eat and shop.

You've Gotta Give This Guy Credit!

After Frank McNamara created Diners Club, a man who worked for a small bank in the New York City area came up with another idea.

William Boyle, an employee at the Franklin Bank in Garden City, Long Island, looked at McNamara's Diners Club card and realized that users had to pay the full balance on the card each month.

Boyle went to his superiors in 1951 and convinced them to issue a credit card that would give customers the option of making just partial payments each month. In effect, it would be an easy loan on which the bank could collect interest on unpaid balances.

The folks at Franklin Bank agreed with Boyle, and created the first revolving-payment credit cards.

Naturally, other banks took notice. The credit card revolution—and habit—was on its way.

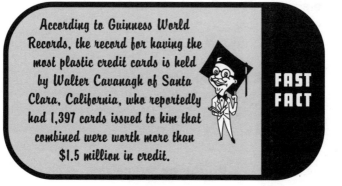

According to Guinness World Records, the record for having the most plastic credit cards is held by Walter Cavanagh of Santa Clara, California, who reportedly had 1,397 cards issued to him that combined were worth more than $1.5 million in credit.

FAST FACT

Name Change

The first credit cards were limited to local areas. Joseph Williams, an executive at California's Bank of America, decided to change these restrictions.

Williams pioneered a statewide card called the BankAmericard. Gradually it was licensed to banks in other states. But by 1976, many issuing banks wanted a different name for the cards. They decided on Visa and Master Charge. Master Charge was later changed to the now-familiar MasterCard.

Credit card historians generally call Joseph Williams the father of today's most-used national cards. Others followed, including the original Diners Club, Carte Blanche, and Discover cards. And you can't forget American Express.

American Express began as the American Express Transportation Company in 1850. They eventually dropped *Transportation* from their name, and issued the first American Express cards in 1958.

Paper or Plastic?

When credit cards first appeared in the early 1950s, they were made of paper.

The now famous plastic cards weren't produced until 1959.

Those first plastic cards were made by American Express; other companies quickly copied the idea.

Plastic cards had three big advantages. They were less likely to be damaged by consumers, they were easier to process in merchants' terminals, and most important, they were less vulnerable to counterfeiting.

Credit cards started a buying revolution. Today people can roam the world armed with nothing more than a piece of plastic, and obtain access to hotels and restaurants, purchase clothes, food, and entertainment with once-unimaginable ease.

Amazingly, Americans now charge more than $1 trillion on credit cards each year.

The biggest single purchase by credit card was made by art collector Eli Broad of Los Angeles, who bought a painting for $2.5 million and charged it to his card.

Think of all the frequent-flier miles he got.

FAST FACT

A Real Tongue Twister

Ruth Fertel was a thirty-eight-year-old New Orleans divorcee who was looking for a business she could buy to help support herself and her two sons.

Checking the classified listings in 1965, she saw an ad from Chris Matulich, who wanted to sell his restaurant. Although she had no previous experience in the food business, Ruth was confident she'd be successful. She mortgaged her house to raise the $18,000 purchase price and became the new owner of the Chris Streak House.

All went well. In fact it went so well that Ruth decided to open a second Chris Steak House. That's when some trouble started.

A second Chris Steak House prompted a legal challenge from Chris Matulich. The solution was for Ruth to add her name to his, creating the tongue-twisting Ruth's Chris Steak House.

Ruth was not happy with the name. In fact she was quoted as saying she hated it, but later said, "We've worked around it."

Still, it's unusual to have a brand name that's so hard to say. However, the cumbersome Ruth's Chris name apparently hasn't hurt business. Before her death in 2002, Ruth had enlarged her chain via franchising to almost 100 locations across America.

Coming to America

One of the strangest gifts the United States ever received resulted in a famous brand name for a learning and research center and museum.

An English scientist, James Smithson, gave his fortune to the United States to establish the Smithsonian Institution.

What made the gift strange—and unexpected—was that Smithson had never been to America and had no ties with the country.

But he was angry at the British upper classes. He thought members of British high society didn't respect him or accept him socially. In retaliation, Smithson left all of his money to the U.S. Congress for "the creation of a scientific institution." As a result, Washington, D.C. is home to the Smithsonian Institution today.

The "World Almanac" got its name not because it contained world facts, but because it was published originally by a newspaper called the "New York World." The book took the name "World Almanac" to promote the paper.

FAST FACT

The Name Can
Be Deceiving

Despite its name, the *Encyclopedia Britannica* no longer comes from Britain.

But it did originate there, in Edinburgh, Scotland. It was founded in the eighteenth century by a group that called itself "The Society of Gentlemen."

In 1768 they published the first edition of what was touted as the best encyclopedia in the English-speaking world. The first editor was a man named William Smellie.

For the next 150 years the *Britannica* was a proud product of Britain. But in the early 1900s two American booksellers, Horace Hooper and Walter Jackson, acquired the rights to the encyclopedia and moved its operations to the United States.

In 1943, William Benton, founder of the large New York advertising agency Benton & Bowles, took control and became the publisher of the encyclopedia. After World War II, a separate American company was set up to run the *Britannica* offices, which today are headquartered many miles from Britain—in Chicago, Illinois.

The Brand Name That Isn't

One of the best-known brand names for dictionaries is Webster's, but did you know that *any* dictionary may call itself a "Webster," and many do?

The trademark rights for *Webster's Dictionary* expired years ago, and the name is now in the public domain.

Who was the original Webster? There were two famous Websters in early U.S. history and they are often confused. One was Daniel, who was a powerful U.S. congressman from Massachusetts, the Secretary of State, and a presidential candidate in the early 1800s.

The dictionary Webster was Noah. He was a schoolteacher in Goshen, New York. Noah first gained fame when he compiled a spelling book in the 1780s that eventually sold millions of copies and helped standardize spelling and pronunciation in America.

Then in the early 1800s, Noah Webster published what many considered the best dictionary of its time. Before his death in 1843, Webster updated and enlarged further editions—and his name became synonymous with dictionaries.

The Name Meant Nothing— and Then Everything

Photographic equipment used to be cumbersome, complex, expensive—and utilized mostly by professionals. George Eastman, who was a clerk in a Rochester, New York, bank, took an interest in photography and got the idea of making the art easier and cheaper for amateurs.

In 1888, Eastman developed his revolutionary camera, the relatively simple handheld Kodak. Photography was changed forever.

The Kodak name came about in a somewhat unusual way. Eastman said he was looking for a word that had never been used before—a word that meant nothing, but one he could trademark and own. To create his word, Eastman said he wanted it to start and end with *K* because, he explained, "That's always been a favorite with me. It's a strong, incisive letter." For the rest of his new word, Eastman played around with all sorts of combinations of letters until he arrived at *Kodak*.

Kodak, the made-up word that meant nothing when Eastman coined it, suddenly meant vast wealth for him, and a way for millions of ordinary people to take and enjoy pictures.

What's the Meaning of "66"?

Brothers Frank and L. E. Phillips founded their gasoline company in 1927.

People have since speculated for years as to why they added the number 66 to their brand.

Quite simply, the number kept appearing and they saw it as a good luck sign.

One of America's major highways in those days was the old Route 66 that went from Chicago to Los Angeles. Route 66 would later become well known throughout the country with a long-running TV series by that name, and a popular song ("I get my kicks on Route 66"). Coincidentally, Phillips's first refinery in Oklahoma, and their first gas station in Kansas, were both near Route 66.

But the clincher came when a company executive was testing the gasoline in his car. The car was speeding along and he said to his driver (using a common expression of the day), "This car goes like sixty with our new gas." The driver looked at the speedometer and exclaimed, "Sixty nothing—we're doing sixty-six." At a meeting the next day, the executive reported the conversation and someone asked where it occurred. The reply was, "Near Tulsa, on Route 66." That did it. The Phillips 66 brand was born.

Movie-and
Motel-Magic

Kemmons Wilson of Memphis, Tennessee, piled his family into his car during the summer of 1951 and headed for a long drive to several vacation spots.

Along the way, Wilson was disgusted with the unreliable motel facilities then available. Some were dirty, few had restaurants or pools or activities for the kids, and it was hard to know what you were getting when you pulled into the parking lot.

Unlike today, there weren't a lot of nationally known chains. Wilson saw an opportunity. Back in Memphis after his vacation, he began his plan for clean, child-friendly, family oriented, reliable motels. He went on to build a chain of motels across America.

And the name for his chain? That was easy.

During World War II, a movie came out that Wilson loved. It featured Bing Crosby crooning Irving Berlin's classic song "White Christmas." It so happened that the movie Wilson enjoyed so much had a title that fit perfectly for his motels. The movie was *Holiday Inn*.

Hot off the Presses?

It may sound strange, but the invention of modern air conditioning in the early 1900s wasn't intended for homes and offices.

Instead, it was developed solely for the printing industry. Hot, sticky days made printing difficult, with high humidity impeding the flow of paper in printing presses.

A young engineering graduate from Cornell University, Willis Carrier, came to the rescue. Carrier developed an air conditioning unit in 1901 for a printer in Brooklyn, New York, and became known as the "father of air conditioning."

Additional units were made for other printers—but incredibly, it took years until air conditioning came to homes, offices, and places of entertainment.

The first theater with air conditioning was the Metropolitan Theater in Los Angeles in 1921. Abraham & Strauss in New York became the first air-conditioned department store, also in 1921. The first air-conditioned office building was the Milam building in San Antonio, Texas, in 1928. Air conditioning didn't come to automobiles until the 1939 Packards, and not until the 1950s did it appear in homes on a consistent basis.

That's Weird

Although Carrier became the first air-conditioning brand name after Willis Carrier's invention of modern air cooling, the Carrier Dome in Syracuse, New York—the well-known arena, funded by and named for his company—was curiously not air conditioned when it was built in 1980.

FAST FACT

Movie theaters were second in line (after printing presses) for the air-conditioning movement. In the 1930s, those theaters that installed air conditioning advertised it heavily. In those days many people went to the theaters on hot days not necessarily to see films, but just to cool off.

Legendary Longevity

When the H. J. Heinz Company was looking for a spokesperson for their 9-Lives cat food, they hired an expert: a real cat. They found one they liked in an animal shelter, and named him Morris.

Morris went on national TV for the first time in 1969. He had an independent attitude that cat lovers appreciated. Morris conveyed the message that even the most finicky cat would be pleased with 9-Lives.

A few years later, Morris died, and the folks at Heinz circulated an obituary in the office, never thinking it would go public. But someone tipped off the media, and the news of the cat's passing was picked up by TV stations and newspapers across America.

Much to the surprise of the people at Heinz, Morris's demise became a big story as everywhere, fans of the feline expressed their sympathy. The company replaced the famous cat with a look-alike from another animal shelter and decided to always use a rescued stray whenever they needed a new Morris.

Turns out the finicky feline may have had nine lives indeed.

"You'll Get the News When We Decide to Give It to You"

For the first thirty years or so of television, viewers were able to get news programs only when the networks and their affiliates wanted to broadcast it.

Ted Turner changed all that with his creation of the first twenty-four-hour, all-news network that he called Cable News Network, or CNN. Turner's pioneering CNN entered homes for the first time in 1980. Two years later he added a sister network, CNN Headline News.

Remarkably, early in his adult life, Turner seemed to be an unlikely candidate for fame and fortune. At age twenty-five, he began working for his father, who owned a billboard company in Atlanta. Unfortunately, his dad suffered financial difficulties and committed suicide, leaving the business to Ted.

Seven years later Ted was able to buy a minor UHF television station in Atlanta, Channel 17. The station was losing money, but Ted had an idea. He used a new communications satellite to beam little Channel 17 all over the country to a nationwide cable TV audience. He called it a "super station" and named it WTBS or TBS, the Turner Broadcasting System, helping to spark the growth of cable television.

Titanic Hero Creates an Unsinkable Network

David Sarnoff came to the United States from Minsk, Russia, in 1900 as a poor nine-year-old immigrant. Just twenty-six years later he would give America its first national broadcasting network.

The Sarnoff saga really began on April 14, 1912, when then-twenty-one-year-old David was working as a wireless radio operator in New York City. He picked up word that the Titanic was sinking—and then stayed at his post for seventy-two consecutive hours, helping to direct rescue ships via wireless to the Titanic's site. Other wireless radio stations shut down to avoid interfering with his work. Sarnoff became a national hero.

It's hard to believe now, but at that time radio was seen simply as a way for two people to communicate, not as a medium for broadcasting news, music, and entertainment to millions.

Sarnoff had the larger vision, and in the 1920s helped form a company to make radio receivers, the Radio Corporation of America (RCA). A network followed to broadcast programs around the nation. Sarnoff called it the National Broadcasting Company, now known as NBC.

CBS Goes Through Two Name Changes

When Bill Paley founded CBS in 1927, he called it United Independent Broadcasters. It was then a network of just a few independently owned radio stations.

Curiously, Paley's entry into the broadcasting business began with cigars. His wealthy family owned a cigar company and bought some commercials on a new-fangled thing called *radio* in the early 1920s. The commercials sold a lot of cigars, and Paley was so impressed with the pulling power of this new medium, he decided to leave the family cigar business behind for it.

Shortly after starting United Independent Broadcasters, Paley acquired Columbia Records. Putting both companies under one roof, he changed the name of United Independent Broadcasters to the Columbia Broadcasting System.

But the CBS acronym wasn't used in those years. Announcers always gave the full name: "This is the Columbia Broadcasting System." The use of the initials didn't become common until after World War II, and even then the name was often written with periods (C.B.S.) since it was an abbreviation.

Eventually, the company officially changed to the now-familiar CBS.

Besides CBS, two other early networks also shied away from acronyms. For years NBC was known as the National Broadcasting Company, and ABC was the American Broadcasting Company.

FAST FACT

The Fox, the Goldfish, and the Lion

A menagerie of animal names inspired a new era of motion pictures.

Wilhelm Fried came to America from Hungary in the early 1900s, changed his name to William Fox, and founded Fox Studios. The company became well known for its movies, and in the present day is also famous for its TV division, which includes the Fox network and the Fox News Channel.

The Goldfish who created a brand was Samuel Goldfish, a Polish immigrant who formed a movie-making partnership with Edgar Selwyn. They called it the Goldwyn Company, taking the *Gold* from Goldfish and the *wyn* from Selwyn. Goldfish then did a curious thing. He liked the company's name so much, he adopted it as his own, and went through the rest of his life as Samuel Goldwyn.

At another point in his career, Goldwyn teamed up with Louis B. Mayer and effected a three-way merger with Metro Pictures, thereby creating Metro-Goldwyn-Mayer (MGM).

In turn, MGM created one of the most famous trademarks—a lion that roars before the opening credits of each movie. The idea came from the studio's publicity man, Howard Dietz, who had attended Columbia University (the Columbia mascot is a lion). Producing the lion trademark was a joy for Dietz, a loyal Columbia alumnus.

FAST FACT

Albert Broccoli is the producer who brought the popular James Bond series to the big screen. And, yes, the vegetable broccoli was named after his family as well. Albert Broccoli is a descendant of a prominent Italian farm family that created the cruciferous green vegetable. They modified cauliflower to produce broccoli—and named it after themselves.

Do You Wear
Ralph Lifshitz's Clothing?

Born in the Bronx, New York, Ralph Lifshitz was destined to influence world fashion. But not under his given name.

Ralph Lifshitz changed his name in the mid-1950s to Ralph Lauren. In the 1960s he began his business by designing men's ties—using flamboyant materials and a wide template instead of the narrow, conservative ties that were then common.

Lauren started his business with twenty-six boxes of homemade ties in 1967. By 2000, his retail empire was a $10 billion global enterprise including couture fashion lines, home collections, and popular fragrances.

In addition to his Lifshitz-Lauren switch, Ralph Lauren picked the word Polo for his brand, evoking the name of a sport that, as he said, embodies a world of elegance, old money, and classic style.

Unflattering Name
Becomes Big Brand

A common, though uncomplimentary, term used to disparage an unstable Latin American country is *Banana Republic*. While you might not feel comfortable using the phrase in conversation, a company boldly took that name and rode it to success.

Banana Republic debuted in 1978 as a seller of safari-inspired clothing. Since then it has grown into one of the biggest retailers of casual apparel.

Banana Republic is one of three separate brands of the Gap Company. Gap came along at just the right time, at the start of the casual clothing boom. It was founded by the husband-and-wife team of Donald and Doris Fisher, who sold their first pair of jeans in San Francisco in 1969. Gap now boasts more than 4,000 stores throughout the U.S., Canada, Great Britain, France, Germany, and Japan.

For their third brand, the Fishers picked a much less controversial name than Banana Republic: Old Navy. (Only young sailors could complain about that.)

A Scandalous Rebellion

At the annual Autumn Ball of Griswold Lorillard's country club, all gentlemen were expected to wear formal black tie and tails. It was the Victorian era, after all, and to wear anything else was unthinkable.

One influential member of the exclusive club, however, did think about wearing something else.

Griswold Lorillard, whose family owned Lorillard Tobacco, then a major tobacco company, had heard about England's fashionable Prince of Wales having the tails cut off his formal coat on a trip to one of the outposts of the British Empire. Inspired, Griswold had his own tailor create a tailless black dinner jacket.

When Griswold wore it to the Autumn Ball in 1886, it caused quite a stir. Some older members thought it was scandalous, but some of the younger men congratulated Griswold on his new, more practical jacket, and soon asked their tailors to make them the same kind.

The club where this all took place was named after the small New York town where it was located—Tuxedo Park. And the new formal tailless jacket was named a tuxedo, after the club.

Who was L. L. Bean?

L. L . Bean's parents must have liked the name Leon because they named their son Leon Leonwood Bean.

But Leon Leonwood Bean hardly ever used his two given names. Just about everybody called him L. L. throughout his life.

L. L. loved to roam the backwoods of Maine, and it was there that he got the idea for his first product in 1912. He wanted boots that were both comfortable and waterproof. He asked a shoemaker in his hometown of Freeport, Maine, to develop a special backwoods boot. L. L. was happy with the results and found that other people wanted similar shoes, so decided to offer them for sale through the mail. That was the beginning of a business that now sells more than $1 billion of outdoor products, sporting goods, and clothing every year.

L. L. died in 1967 at age ninety-four, and the L. L. Bean Company was taken over by his grandson. His grandson's last name was Gorman, but you can probably guess his first name: Leon, of course.

His Boyhood Dreams Were Shattered–But He Did Okay

Growing up in Missouri, a young boy excelled at just about everything he tried. He became the youngest Eagle Scout in the state, president of his high school class, and quarterback on the state champion football team. Those achievements led to big dreams. Maybe, he thought, he could be president of the United States some day, or a pro football star, or at least attend a prominent Ivy League college.

None of those things happened. As adulthood approached in 1940, he took a job for $75 a month at a J. C. Penney store in Des Moines, Iowa.

Five years later he ran a store in Newport, Arkansas, and began to learn the art of discounting. From there he opened his own store in Bentonville, Arkansas, calling it Walton's Five and Dime. Selling an increasing number of goods at the lowest possible prices, he continued to open more stores in small towns.

On July 2, 1962, at his store in Rogers, Arkansas, a new company name was used for the first time. Walton's Five and Dime became Wal-Mart. Founder Sam Walton had done pretty well for himself. He was on his way to becoming one of the richest men in the nation. His company would eventually take in more money every year than any American business.

In his first year in the automobile business, Henry Ford went bankrupt. Two years later his second company also failed. On his third try, he was successful. Likewise, R.H. Macy went broke with his first two stores. The third one became famous.

FAST FACT

His Product Made Millions. He Made $400.

One day in 1849, Walter Hunt was fooling around with a piece of wire and came up with a new kind of pin. He called it a dress pin, but the world came to know it as the safety pin.

Hunt patented the safety pin, and that patent went on to be worth millions of dollars. However, shortly after receiving his patent and before the money started rolling in, Hunt sold it for $400 because he owed a man $15 at the time and didn't have the cash. Hunt paid his creditor $15 and was happy to pocket $385.

What's worse, Hunt had invented a sewing machine years before and had thrown away a fortune when he didn't patent it at all. His reason was that he feared it might cause unemployment among seamstresses.

But don't be too worried about Hunt's misfortune. He eventually became rich with his inventions of a fire alarm, knife sharpener, icebreaker, and fountain pen.

Not many people have heard of Hunt, but this New York mechanic was one of history's most unusual and ingenious inventors.

Whatever Happened to Mr. Sears and Mr. Roebuck?

Although the giant Sears, Roebuck and Company was founded by Richard Sears and Alvah Roebuck, neither Sears nor Roebuck stayed around very long.

The famous Sears Roebuck brand started in 1886, when Sears opened a jewelry store in Chicago and teamed up with Roebuck, who was a watchmaker.

After being in business a short time, they got the idea of selling not only watches and jewelry, but other products as well—by mail. In the late 1800s, mail order was big business. Almost two-thirds of Americans lived on farms or in rural areas with no easy access to a variety of stores. Sears and Roebuck began to build what would be the largest mail order company in the world. Later as the U.S. urbanized, Sears Roebuck opened stores around the nation and became a huge corporation—but neither Sears nor Roebuck was still there to see it.

Roebuck, in poor health, left just three years after joining Sears. And as the company grew, requiring more executives and more financing, Sears was forced out in 1908 at age forty-three.

Only their names remain.

So Many Names Until the Right One Came Along

No one's clothing had zippers until the twentieth century, and when zippers were finally made, they weren't called zippers.

The first zipper was invented by Chicago engineer Whitcomb Judson in 1893. He called his zippers—made for boots, not clothing—*clasp-lockers*. But they didn't work too well and faded from the scene.

Next came Norwegian inventor Gordon Sundback, who patented what he called a *slide fastener* in 1917.

Then in 1923 the B. F. Goodrich Company bought 150,000 slide fasteners, or *hookless fasteners* as they were also called, for use on rubber galoshes. Mr. Goodrich himself is credited with coining the name *zippers*, based on the "zip" sound when the slide fasteners were closed.

Surprisingly, zippers on clothing didn't become common until the 1930s, when fly fronts on men's pants slowly changed from buttons to zippers. Zippers soon began to appear on women's dresses as well.

When a man puts on a shirt, the buttons are on his right, while on most women's garments, the buttons are usually on the left. Why? Men traditionally dressed themselves, and since most people are right-handed, it's easier to grasp the button in the right hand to put it through a buttonhole. But when the custom started, many fashionable women were dressed by maids, who naturally faced their mistresses while buttoning them up.

FAST FACT

India Gave Us Khakis and Dungarees

British soldiers stationed in their former territory of India in the 1800s were ordered to wear dust-colored uniforms for camouflage in the dusty terrain. The Hindi word for dust is *khaki*, so it didn't take long for the uniforms to be called *khakis*. Also, a type of British blue jeans were made in the Indian city of Dungri—and became known as *dungarees*.

What Does "Nasdaq" Stand For?

Anybody who follows national news hears or sees the word *Nasdaq* all the time. Although it's familiar enough, it's surprising how few people can tell you exactly what *Nasdaq* means.

Nasdaq is actually an acronym. The first four initials aren't too hard to figure out: They stand for National Association of Securities Dealers. But what do those last two initials denote?

The *a* stands for *automated* and the *q* for *quotations.*

The trading network originally was known by its full name, the National Association of Securities Dealers Automated Quotations. Now the preferred name is, simply, Nasdaq, with no periods indicating the abbreviations nor capital letters except for the *N.*

Although stock markets started in the early days of the United States, Nasdaq didn't begin operations until 1971. Nonetheless, it is now the second-biggest market in the country after the New York Stock Exchange.

The Homeless Stock Markets

It's hard to imagine today, but when the prestigious New York Stock Exchange was founded in 1792, it met every business day on a sidewalk under a buttonwood tree on Wall Street. Rain, snow, or shine, members of the exchange traded stocks outside. The exchange had no indoor home of its own.

The American Stock Exchange started the same way—and stayed outside until 1921. That exchange went by the name of New York Curb Exchange because all their trading was done—literally—on the curbs of sidewalks. Their name didn't change from the Curb Exchange to the American Stock Exchange until 1953, even though they had moved inside thirty-two years before.

The Amazing Aluminum Coincidence

In 1886, Charles Hall of Thompson, Ohio, discovered the process that made production of aluminum practical, and he formed the Aluminum Company of America, which later turned into the well-known Alcoa.

At the same time a man named Paul Heroult was working in Paris. He discovered the same process in the same year as Hall, even though they worked independently of each other and didn't know of each others' activities. Heroult set up a European aluminum company.

What makes the coincidence even greater is that both Hall and Heroult were born in 1863; both discovered the aluminum process in 1886; both set up their own companies to manufacture aluminum in 1888; and both died in 1914.

An Advertising First

The first commercial ever broadcast over a radio station was for the Queensboro Realty Company on station WEAF in New York in 1922. Radio broadcasting was already two years old before anyone thought of putting advertisements on the air.

When broadcasting started in 1920, most stations were owned by radio manufacturers. They expected to make money by selling more radios. It took two years until somebody realized money could be made by selling commercials on the air.

As for television advertising, there was none until 1939, when one of the early experimental stations, W2XBS, a forerunner of WNBC in New York, aired a commercial for Ivory Soap during a baseball telecast. That was the start.

The Most Underrated Product

Not many people think of the telegraph as one of history's most exciting inventions, but it gave humans something significant they had never had before.

Until the telegraph was invented in 1844, people had no way to communicate instantly over any great distance. The telephone, radio, and TV were still years away.

The telegraph was the first instant long-distance communication system—and was really one of the landmark creations of all time.

An oddity about the telegraph is that its inventor, Samuel Morse, spent much of his early career in a field far removed from science. Morse had studied art and became a portrait painter, then worked as a professor of painting at New York University in 1832.

While on the faculty, he became interested in uses of electricity and began experimenting with the possibility of using it to send messages. Twelve years later he gave the world the telegraph.

FAST FACT

Although the Morse Code series of dots and dashes used by telegraphers was obviously named after inventor Samuel Morse, Morse himself didn't invent the code. It was created by telegraph executive Alfred Vail.

The Slow Growth of TV

Although there were several experimental television stations in the late 1930s as television technology became more practical, the manufacture of sets was severely curtailed by World War II. It wasn't until after the war that television became a mass medium, but it was still slow to take off. As late as 1948, only two percent of American homes had TV sets. The first coast-to-coast television programming in America started in 1951. Color TV began in 1953.

Boy Wonders

Credit youth for the creation of both radio and television.

When Guglielmo Marconi invented radio in 1895, he was not yet twenty-one years of age. And one of the key principles that made television possible was developed by a high school student, Philo Farnsworth.

Marconi, who was from a wealthy family in Bologna, Italy, never attended school. He was educated at home by private tutors and began experimenting with radio transmission, or wireless telegraphy, as a teenager. He perfected it by the time he was twenty years old, sending the first signals from a transmitter he built at his father's estate.

In 1922, at age sixteen, Farnsworth, who was from Beaver, Utah, worked on experiments to send pictures through the air. He found a way to do it with his discovery of what he called an *image dissector*. At the urging of his high school principal, Farnsworth sold his invention to RCA, where it played an important part in the creation of TV.

FAST FACT

When teenage TV inventor Philo Farnsworth became an adult, he hated television programming so much that he stopped watching it altogether. He refused to have a TV set in his house.

The Brand That Was First on Network Radio & TV

When the first national radio network, NBC, went on the air one evening in 1926, an announcer read its first commercial: "It's 8:00 P.M., B-U-L-O-V-A, Bulova Watch time.

The Bulova Watch Company had made advertising history—and used that same pioneering radio commercial format for years afterward. The commercials helped make Bulova a major brand. The company got its name from its founder, Joseph Bulova, who was a twenty-three-year-old immigrant from Bohemia who had opened a small jewelry store in New York City in 1875. Bulova prospered, and by 1911 he began manufacturing clocks and watches.

On July 1, 1941 the company made broadcast history again with the first commercial on network TV. It showed a picture of a clock and a map of the United States. An announcer said, "America runs on Bulova time." That commercial cost Bulova about $9 (a small price for a place in television history).

Before the 1900s, most people never wore wristwatches. Men carried pocket watches, and women often attached watch fobs to their dresses. But during World War I, the Army issued wristwatches to soldiers for quicker access to time, and when vets returned home they brought wristwatches back and popularized them.

FAST FACT

Talk, Talk, Talk

When radio was the major broadcasting medium in the 1920s and 1930s, all stations were on the AM, or amplitude modulation, band.

Then Edwin Armstrong found another method of sending radio signals. He started an experimental station in Alpine, New Jersey, in 1939, using FM, or frequency modulation.

The advantage of FM was that its signal was clearer and less interfered by static. It was especially good for transmission of music. Its disadvantage compared to AM was that its signal didn't go as far.

The growth and acceptance of FM was slow because existing radio sets couldn't receive it. People had to buy new, special radios to get FM.

It wasn't until the 1950s that manufacturers began mass-marketing FM radios, and more and more stations began broadcasting on the FM band.

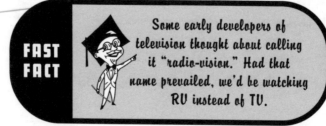

FAST FACT

Some early developers of television thought about calling it "radio-vision." Had that name prevailed, we'd be watching RV instead of TV.

How Cable TV Started

In 1947, John Walson of Mahanoy City, Pennsylvania, owned an appliance store.

He was having trouble selling television sets because the mountains of eastern Pennsylvania interfered with reception.

So Walson got an idea. He built an antenna on top of a nearby mountain and ran a cable to TV sets in his store window.

Walson then persuaded residents to hook up to his cable system in their homes for a $100 installation fee and $2 a month.

Reception was good, and Walson sold a lot of television sets.

He eventually owned a large cable TV company in Pennsylvania and New Jersey, and was recognized by the National Cable TV Association in 1979 as the pioneer of cable TV.

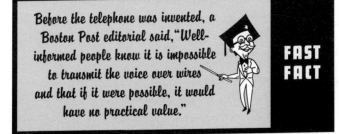

Before the telephone was invented, a Boston Post editorial said, "Well-informed people know it is impossible to transmit the voice over wires and that if it were possible, it would have no practical value."

FAST FACT

It Might Not Have Been the Bell Telephone Company

Although we've always heard that Alexander Graham Bell was the inventor of the telephone, at least two other inventors contested that claim.

Elisha Gray filed a patent for a telephone the same day as Bell, but lost out in a bitter lawsuit. Part of Gray's problem was that he filed for his patent two hours after Bell.

And Daniel Drawbaugh insisted he invented a telephone several years before Bell. Drawbaugh came close to convincing the U.S. Supreme Court, losing to Bell by a 4-3 decision.

Thus, instead of the Bell Telephone Company, we might have had the Gray or the Drawbaugh Telephone Company.

Surprisingly, Bell didn't set out to invent the telephone in the first place. His wife and mother were both hearing impaired, and Bell was working on machines to help hard-of-hearing people hear better. Those experiments coincidentally led to the telephone.

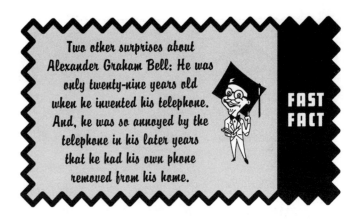

Two other surprises about Alexander Graham Bell: He was only twenty-nine years old when he invented his telephone. And, he was so annoyed by the telephone in his later years that he had his own phone removed from his home.

FAST FACT

The Rainbow Pages

The color of the Yellow Pages was not chosen intentionally. A printer in Cheyenne, Wyoming, was printing business listings in the back of a phone book, when the printer ran out of white paper. He was forced to use some yellow stock paper he happened to have on hand. The phone company liked the change and started routinely using yellow pages around the country, eventually trademarking the name Yellow Pages.

Little Girl Is Over Fifty Years Old—
But Hasn't Aged a Bit

One of the most popular and enduring symbols for a brand—a cocker spaniel tugging at the bathing suit of a little pigtailed girl—was first used by Coppertone suntan lotion in 1953.

The idea for the girl and the dog was a collaborative idea of Coppertone executives and the Embry ad agency of Miami.

The picture of the girl, who became known as Little Miss Coppertone, was modeled after the daughter of one of the illustrators. She and her dog began appearing on billboards, in magazine and newspaper ads, on walls of buildings, and on bottles of Coppertone. A fourteen-by-sixty-foot billboard featuring an animation of a twenty-foot tall Little Miss Coppertone and a mechanical dog trying to pull down her suit was a landmark for thirty five years at the Golden Glades interchange in Miami.

And Little Miss Coppertone was joined by some famous friends. A 1966 TV commercial featured a future movie star, then three-year-old Jodie Foster, in her professional acting debut.

Those Versatile Jacuzzi Brothers

The seven Jacuzzi brothers, who emigrated to California from Italy in the early 1900s, liked to build things.

Shortly after arriving in the United States they built the first enclosed cabin for an airplane. Their plane was used to carry U.S. mail and some passengers within California.

Then the brothers switched to making agricultural pumps and opened a business under the name of the Jacuzzi Brothers Deep Well Pump Company.

But what started them on the path of having their name become world famous was when one of their relatives began suffering from arthritis in 1956. To help treat the arthritis, they designed a hydrotherapy pump, then made them for hospitals.

A third-generation member of the family, Roy Jacuzzi, took that product one step further in 1968. He invented the first self-contained, fully integrated whirlpool bath, incorporating jets into the sides of a tub. Roy had created a new industry and a new brand name—the Jacuzzi.

Teachers Teach Us About Health Insurance

The first health insurance brand name and plan in America was started by a sympathetic former school superintendent in Texas in 1929.

Justin Kimball, the superintendent of Dallas schools and an official at Baylor University, wondered how he could help teachers cope with medical costs.

His solution was to work out a deal with a university hospital. The hospital would guarantee health care to each teacher in exchange for teachers making a regular monthly payment.

It was a revolutionary concept—and one that is now recognized as America's first health insurance plan.

For its name, the plan wanted something that connoted an organization helping people, like the Red Cross. They couldn't use Red Cross so they called it Blue Cross. All other brand name health plans and HMOs followed.

Medicare did not exist in the United States until 1966.

FAST FACT

What's Wrong with this Brand Name?

The Great Atlantic & Pacific Tea Company, started in 1869, was the first chain-store operation in America. It was a strange choice for a name. First of all, hardly anybody used its formal name. Just about everybody called it the A&P. Secondly, their stores sold a lot more than tea. They were fully stocked grocery stores.

And third, it took the company fifty years to live up to its name and place stores on both the Atlantic and Pacific coasts.

Whatever It's Called, Don't Squeeze It

When the Hoberg Paper Company of Green Bay, Wisconsin began manufacturing a new brand of especially soft toilet paper in 1928, one of their employees said the paper was "charming." The company left the g off *charming* and gave us the name *Charmin*. They also changed the pronunciation from *char-min* to *shar-min*.

FAST FACT

What do monkey wrenches have to do with monkeys? Nothing. Their name comes from inventor Charles Monke of England, who made the first one.

The Cart That Changed the World

Many of those brand-name products you buy are placed in "The Cart That Changed the World." That is what the shopping cart is called in the biography of its inventor, Sylvan Goldman.

As Goldman watched shoppers at his grocery store in Oklahoma City in 1936, he got his inspiration. He noticed that customers didn't buy as many products as they might because they could only carry so many items up to the checkout counter. In those days some shoppers brought baskets with them, but the baskets quickly became too full or too heavy.

With the help of a carpenter and a maintenance man, Goldman built the first grocery cart and patented it. He formed the Folding Carrier Company to manufacture it, and became a millionaire.

Goldman's shopping cart was soon being used by stores everywhere and was a major development in the history of merchandising.

Call the Doctor

Whenever radio talk-show hosts have a nagging question they need answered, or want some entertaining, surprising stories for their show, they call Charles Reichblum, the author of the *Knowledge in a Nutshell®* books.

Because of Reichblum's vast trove of fun facts and stories, which he's accrued over fifty years, it's only natural that those radio talkers gave him the nickname Dr. Knowledge™.

Reichblum has even taken his brand name one step further by hosting his own *Dr. Knowledge™ Show* on Pittsburgh radio station KDKA. And he's now the author of the amazing *Dr. Knowledge™* books published by Black Dog & Leventhal.

A graduate of Syracuse University, Reichblum served as president of the Century Features news service for forty years. He wrote his first book, *Greatest Events in American History*, which won a Freedoms Foundation Award, in 1966.

He lives in Pittsburgh, amid the thousands of newspaper clippings and computer printouts about fascinating, surprising, and amazing facts that just keep growing all the time.

The Skinny
on America . . . and
Its Brands

1776-1799 Americans win the Revolutionary War and get their democratic form of government from the Founding Fathers—but enjoy none of the pleasures and conveniences of today's products and brands. Cooking on wood-burning stoves is an all-day affair in most homes. (No quick call for a pizza; there are no phones and no pizza stores.) Many homemakers spend hours scrubbing clothes (no electric washers and dryers; no electricity). Treats like candy and cookies, and necessities like soap and candles are mostly homemade. Got a headache? A home remedy is concocted, for there's no aspirin or Tylenol. Need an antibiotic or something for a cut or burn? Try vinegar. Surgery necessary? Unfortunately, there's no modern anesthetic. Sometimes liquor or certain herbs are tried, but they don't do much good. Great pain and, often, shock result. Want to communicate with a distant friend or relative? Three choices: Hitch up a horse, get in a boat, or write a letter, which might get to its destination… but who knows when.

1800-1809 The nation's capital moves to Washington, D.C. President Thomas Jefferson completes the Louisiana Purchase from France, which doubles the area of the United States and greatly increases the economic potential of the country. Lewis and Clark begin their expedition to explore the new American west—and the first of today's familiar brand names appears as William Colgate arrives in America from England and opens a much-needed soap and candle manufacturing company in New York City. A new era in better transportation begins as Robert Fulton's steamboat completes a successful maiden voyage from New York City to Albany.

1810-1819 The United States census shows a population of just over seven million for the nation, fewer people than today's population of just one city, New York. With no supermarkets and many people living far from any kind of store (which has limited supplies, if it even exists), how do folks put food on the family table? They get it from their own farms or from ones close by, and most people grow at least their own fruits and vegetables in home gardens. A big problem is food preservation, necessary in order to get through those times when supplies are not plentiful. Homemakers learn to salt, pickle, smoke, and can foods to keep them usable year round.

1820-1829 A minister who preaches about healthy eating gives his name to a new product that's still around today: The graham cracker is named for the Reverend Sylvester Graham. The first passenger railroad in the nation, the Baltimore & Ohio, begins operations. A strike by weavers in Pawtucket, Rhode Island, is the first such action by women. The Erie Canal, an important waterway for shipping goods to and from the Midwest and East Coast, opens. A famous brand name for dictionaries is established as Noah Webster publishes his best-selling *American Dictionary of the English Language*.

1830-1839 One of the best-known and longest-lasting brand names is created when brothers-in-law William

Procter and James Gamble open the Procter & Gamble Company in Cincinnati, Ohio. Like William Colgate, who founded his company earlier, Procter and Gamble make soap and candles, relieving many homemakers of the time-consuming and tedious task of making them at home. Oberlin College in Ohio becomes the first to offer degrees to both men and women. The Liberty Bell cracks while tolling the death of Chief Justice John Marshall, creating a memorable American symbol.

1840-1849 This milestone decade sees the creation of many products that are taken for granted today. Elias Howe invents the sewing machine. Samuel Morse invents the telegraph and wires, "What hath God wrought" from Washington to Baltimore, the first instant message capable of traveling a distance of many miles. Walter Hunt invents the safety pin. Hanson Gregory puts the hole in doughnuts. Austin Church and John Dwight found the Church & Dwight Company that's still around and is famous now for its Arm & Hammer brand. Ether and chloroform are used successfully as anesthetics—first by dentists, then by surgeons during operations. The first U.S. adhesive postage stamps appear with a five-cent Benjamin Franklin and a ten-cent George Washington. Gold is discovered in California, sending thousands west in search of riches.

1850-1859 Among those flocking to the California gold rush is young immigrant named Levi Strauss, who begins making denim work clothes for the miners. George Crum creates the potato chip. Navy commander Mathew Perry negotiates a treaty with Japan to open trade with the United States. The first railroad train crosses the Mississippi River, going from Rock Island, Illinois, to Davenport, Iowa. The oil industry breaks first ground in the United States when Edwin Drake drills the nation's first commercially successful oil well in Titusville, Pennsylvania. Frederick Miller arrives from Germany and opens a small brewery in Milwaukee that makes, appropriately, Miller Beer.

1860-1869 Henry John Heinz opens the H. J. Heinz Company, and makes a number of condiments, of which, surprisingly, ketchup is not the first (it's horseradish—ketchup follows later). Adolphus Busch marries Eberhard Anheuser's daughter, and the Anheuser-Busch brand is born. The first college football game is played and Rutgers beats Princeton, 6-4. The Pony Express begins service between St. Joseph, Missouri, and Sacramento, California. Southern states secede from the Union to form the Confederate States of America and the Civil War is fought between 1861 and 1865. *The World Almanac* is published for the first time. The Great Atlantic & Pacific Tea Company, better known as the A&P, opens with one store in New York.

1870-1879 The telephone makes its appearance as Alexander Graham Bell receives his patent. America gets electric lights and inventor Thomas Edison founds the Edison Electric Light Company, forerunner of General Electric. F. W. Woolworth opens a store in Utica, New York—the first five-and-ten. Adolph Coors starts his brewery in Golden, Colorado. A different kind of beer—root beer—is introduced by Charles Hires in Philadelphia. As more Americans get indoor bathrooms, the Scott brothers market the first commercial toilet paper. One of the earliest home remedies that's still manufactured today is sold for the first time: Vaseline.

1880-1889 The first long-distance telephone call is made from New York to Boston. The soft drink industry grows as Coca-Cola and Dr Pepper are invented. George Eastman makes picture-taking easy with his Kodak camera. Saltwater taffy and candy corn are introduced to America's sweet teeth. Charles Dow sends out mimeographed business news reports; soon he'll use a newspaper format and call it *The Wall Street Journal*. Dr. Joseph Lister pioneers antiseptic surgery in England. A new product that's advertised to kill "million of germs" in the mouth and prevent bad breath is named after Dr. Lister and put on sale in America as Listerine. With new products beginning to make life somewhat easier, and with the industrial revolution bringing more people from farms to cities, Americans have more time for recreation. As a result, new centers of entertainment appear: vaudeville theaters abound, the first roller coaster in the United States opens at Coney Island, New York, and baseball begins to grow in popularity as the nation's favorite pastime.

1890-1899 The Age of the Automobile dawns as the first cars go on sale in Springfield, Massachusetts, by the Duryea brothers. Milton Hershey makes his first Hershey chocolate bar, which becomes the first national candy brand. At the Chicago World's Fair, then called the Columbian Exposition, Cracker Jack and Ferris wheels are seen for the first time. The first motion pictures are shown by Thomas Edison's kinetoscope. Many of today's well-known products and brands are created, including Jell-O, Fig Newtons, Dole, Pepsi-Cola, Smuckers, Bengay, aspirin, and Wrigley's chewing gum. The Spanish-American War makes the United States a world power.

1900-1909 The Wright brothers show humans can fly with their maiden airplane voyage. The first movie to tell a story, *The Great Train Robbery*, is released. (Earlier movies simply showed unrelated scenes.) Three major events lead to the first federal food safety laws: a book by Upton Sinclair, *The Jungle*, which exposes filthy conditions in the meat-packing industry; the development of microbiology; and the realization by some manufacturers that unless food safety is monitored, consumers will lose confidence in their products. In 1906, Congress passes the landmark Pure Food and Drug Act. Ready-to-eat breakfast cereal is introduced by William Kellogg. (Before that many homemakers had to cook goodies like oatmeal for hours in order to put cereals on their table.) Animal Crackers make their debut. King Gillette revolutionizes shaving with safety razors and disposable blades. Henry Ford's Model T makes autos affordable for many. Hot dogs get their name from a newspaper cartoonist. Modern air conditioning is invented, although it doesn't become common in homes for fifty more years. At the St. Louis World's Fair the ice cream cone and iced tea are born.

1910-1919 America enters World War I. The income tax is made legal. On a happier note, the world's best-selling cookie—the Oreo—debuts. Henry Ford makes news when he raises wages of his workers to $5 for an eight-hour day. The *Titanic* sinks and telegraph operator David Sarnoff proves the value of the wireless, which will soon turn into radio. Stores of the first supermarket chain, the Piggly Wiggly, open in Memphis, Tennessee. Planters peanuts introduces its beloved and enduring symbol, Mr. Peanut. The Prohibition Constitutional Amendment is ratified, banning the manufacture and sale of alcoholic beverages.

1920-1929 Peace and prosperity come to America. It's the decade of a new medium: radio. KDKA, Pittsburgh, goes on the air; other stations follow and NBC and CBS are created. Wonder bread, Wheaties, popsicles, drive-in restaurants, Q-tips, Kleenex, Band-Aids, and Scotch Tape are all born as is the beloved little rodent Mickey Mouse. Women get the right to vote in national elections. *Time* magazine and *Reader's Digest* are published. Talkies replace silent movies with Al Jolson's *The Jazz Singer*. The stock market crash of October 29, 1929, ends the Roaring Twenties and ushers in the Great Depression. The show business paper *Variety* marks the event with its classic headline "Wall Street Lays an Egg."

1930-1939 President Franklin Roosevelt closes all banks in March 1933; only those in sound condition are allowed to reopen. Despite the Depression, new brand launches include Krispy Kreme, Sara Lee, Spam, Toll House, and Pepperidge Farm. Whiskey, wine, and beer flow again as Prohibition ends after a thirteen-year experiment. Congress passes the Social Security Act. Explosion of the air ship *Hindenburg* ends dirigible passenger service. Shopping carts, electric razors, FM radio, airline stewardesses, the Monopoly board game, soap operas, and Superman all enter the scene.

1940-1949 Japan bombs Pearl Harbor and the United States enters World War II. Pay-as-you-go income tax featuring withholding on paychecks is initiated. At the end of World War II in 1945, the Baby Boom begins. Another boom begins as television sets enter American homes in increasing numbers. M&M candy goes on sale for the first time. Two brothers named McDonald open a single hamburger stand in San Bernardino, California, and Glen Bell opens a hot dog stand from which he'll soon sell tacos and rename Taco Bell. Frozen foods and microwave cooking are in their infancy but will soon have major impact on kitchens across America.

1950-1959 A significant development in product purchasing comes to the nation with the creation and widespread acceptance of credit cards. Americans buy television sets in record numbers and gather around the tube with new pre-packaged meals called TV dinners. Little girls get a grown-up doll named Barbie. The first Pizza Hut and Burger King open. The U.S. surgeon general issues the first report showing a link between cigarette smoking and lung cancer. Airplane travel is brought to the masses with the advent of coach class. Jet passenger service begins on a National Airlines flight from New York to Miami.

1960-1969 Medicare is inaugurated. The first Super Bowl is played and its name is coined by the eight-year-old daughter of NFL owner Lamar Hunt, who had been play-ing with a popular toy of the time—a super ball. Neil Armstrong becomes the first human to walk on the moon. The first Wendy's, Domino's, and Subway fast-food restau-rants open. Diet drinks and Gatorade are introduced. The country begins to change as the civil rights movement, the movement for equal rights for women, a youth rebel-lion against old-style authority, and a transition toward casual dress all get under way.

1970-1979 Although some "experts" had predicted that computers would only be used by big businesses, twen-ty-one-year old Steve Jobs and twenty-five-year-old Steve Wozniak build a personal computer under their Apple brand that will soon help fuel a revolution with PCs in homes and offices everywhere. Another revolution occurs in overnight package delivery as Fred Smith starts FedEx, and Ted Turner transforms cable TV by using a satellite to beam programming across the country. An oil embargo against the United States drives up gas prices, which aids a major influx of smaller Japanese cars into the American market. A new stock exchange, Nasdaq, debuts and will help finance the coming dot-com boom.

1980-1989 In a settlement of a milestone lawsuit by the Justice Department, AT&T, which had become the biggest company in the world, agrees to give up its twenty-two Bell System companies. It's the biggest breakup since Standard Oil was split into separate companies in 1911. After introducing the unsuccessful New Coke to the mar-ket, Coca-Cola quickly backs away from it and vows to continue marketing its traditional drink, renamed Coca-Cola Classic. The boys at Apple do it again, popularizing the use of the mouse for navigating a computer. Microsoft makes the big time, licensing its operating system to IBM. Michael Dell starts Dell computers. Starbucks opens its first coffee bar in Seattle. Ted Turner strikes again with the first all-news TV channel, CNN. And those partially sticky Post-it notes appear in all sorts of places.

1990-Present Familiar names like Amazon.com, Google, Yahoo!, eBay, and even World Wide Web are all coined in the 1990s. A food industry revolution takes place in 1990 when, for the first time, the U.S. government mandates that all companies list the contents and nutritional values of foods in a standardized way on all packages, jars, and cans. A different kind of transformation occurs politically as the once-feared Soviet Union crumbles in 1991, not only effectively ending the Cold War, but leaving America the world's predominant superpower. A beautiful September morning in 2001 ushers in a new and unsettling era as terrorists crash hijacked airliners into physical symbols of U.S. economic and military might. Despite the trying times, Americans continue to invent new ideas, concepts, and brands undreamed of by their countrymen who founded the nation more than 200 years before.